GUIDANCE THROUGH

The Care-Giving Journey

Into the World of Dementia

Paulette Kozlowski RN CDP ADC

Copyright © 2023 by Paulette Kozlowski LLC

All rights reserved. No part of this book may be reproduced or transmitted in any form or by any means without written permission from the author.

ISBN: XXXXXXXXXXXXX

Visit the web: www.Guidance4Dementia.com

THIS BOOK IS DEDICATED:

To all those who have been afflicted with a brain injury or a dementing Illness,

To those who devote time and energy to care for those afflicted,

To My own Family – A Family of Caregivers,

To the thousands of CAREGIVERS, I have met throughout my career, to the hundreds I have worked with, and to those who have agreed to share some of their caregiving experiences in this book,

To the former First Lady Rosalyn Carter

who understood the value of caregiving and ESTABLISHED AN INSTITUTE to promote the health, education, strength, and resilience of caregivers throughout the United States,

And last but not least, to all of the wonderful people I have had the opportunity to work with for the past 20 years at the St. Johns County Council on Aging Inc. in St. Augustine, Florida. This includes my phenomenally devoted, hardworking, and caring Nocatee and Sunshine Center staff whom I am so proud and grateful for as they provide such tender loving care to all of our very special participants each and every day. I also want to acknowledge all of the outstanding board members, Executive director, Financial director, Program director, Managers, Coordinators, and all of

JOURNEY

our other devoted employees, and volunteers. It is truly an honor and a pleasure to work with such an exceptionally talented and caring team as we strive to help improve the lives of those we serve.

TABLE OF CONTENTS

Acknowledgments 1
Forward 6
Preparing for the Journey: 9
Trail Marker 1 The Journey starts with Me (the Caregiver) 16
Trail Marker #2 Learning to Accept – 26

   Learning to Retrain Your Brain 26

Trail Marker #3: Learning to Let Go….............................. 38
Trail Marker # 4: Learning to Understand 42

   Climbing a Mountain of Education & Enlightenment .. 42

Trail Marker # 5 Descending Down the Mountain – 74

   Through the Stages 74

Trail Marker 6. Through the Rough Terrain 91

   Learning to deal with Difficult Challenges 91

Trail Marker 7 Learning to Be Kind to Yourself 115

   Finding Peace and Harmony 115

Journey's End. Preparing for the final journey Home 124

ACKNOWLEDGMENTS

What a privilege it has been to have had the opportunity to meet, work with, admire, and learn from so many wonderful patients and their families throughout my 50-year nursing career. During most of those years, I was given the opportunity to work closely with persons whose lives have been forever changed due to brain disease or injury. As a nurse educator, I have also had the opportunity to travel alongside and guide many caregivers throughout their dementia care journey. Together we often learned from and mentored each other along the way. Their number is so great that it would take another entire book to list all of the names of those deserving a dedication. So many people have played a role in writing this book without even knowing it. Since space is limited, instead of listing each name, I list their title as "Caregivers" and "Loved Ones". Several of the caregivers have consented to share a small part of their lives and experiences on this journey with you; in hopes that you too will be able to learn from their experiences. Their stories are true while their names and some of the surroundings have been changed to protect their privacy. I also dedicate this book to the loved ones they cared for; some of whom I had the privilege of sharing great times with as well as learning from in Adult Day Care Programs. It is amazing how much you can learn about what it's like to live in the dementia world if you stop to take the time to really connect with someone living there and delve into their deepest feelings. Once connected, it usually doesn't take long to discover ways to bring out smiles and help them find happiness once again in spite of the changes they are facing. These wonderful and special people deserve the highest dedication, as they played the greatest part in the context of this book.

I am also proud to say, that I was privileged to have been born into a line of family caregivers. Therefore, I want to give special mention to the following:

My grandparents, Mae and Jack Lucas with whom I had the honor of spending many summers in their home making wonderful memories throughout my childhood. They became shared caregivers of my great-grandma Kolar after my great-grandfather passed away. I recall watching old movies of her happily dancing in her later years. She developed vascular dementia but managed to live a full and happy life in spite of it.

My parents Jeannette and John Moran. I was so fortunate to have been born and raised by such a loving couple. They were childhood sweethearts and that love never faded. I was the middle child of 5 children. After my grandfather Lukas passed away, my parents became caregivers to my grandmother Mae, who was in her 80s. I lived a few houses away from them at the time and was able to spend special moments once again with my grandmother. We bowled together every week on a women's bowling league. She too, like her mother before her, had a history of heart disease, and in her 90s vascular dementia set in. She was still able to enjoy life in spite of it.

To all of my siblings and my Husband Dennis: When my father passed away, my mother remained in her home in Michigan for several years. My oldest brother helped her out when needed, as he and his wife lived next door. During the winters my mother enjoyed taking turns living with her other

4 children. When it was time to no longer live alone, she spent much of her time with my youngest sister and her husband in her hometown of Ohio. My youngest brother drove several miles out of his way, to pick mom up and take her to breakfast at least once a week. He wanted her to know how much she meant to him and his family. She enjoyed many a holiday at their dinner table. In the winter mom would enjoy living with my oldest sister and her husband in Georgia.

I was privileged to have spent the last 3 years of my mother's life with her as she chose to live with me and my husband in Florida. At that point, she became not only my mother but my best friend. We shared many similar interests and experiences together. Unfortunately, she too, had a history of heart disease which started to affect her circulation and strength. MCI (Mild Cognitive Impairment) began to set in at the age of 93. I found that my previous education and experience worked amazingly well for us. Toward the end of her last year of life, forgetfulness, balance problems, and generalized weakness all became a normal part of our lives. We were able to enjoy and be thankful for every moment spent together in spite of it.

We as a family, were blessed with the fact that mom asked and chose to live with all of us. Some families are not so lucky in this area. Many elders find it very difficult to leave their homes. It took a while after my father died, but my mother realized one day, that it was time to move on. Living alone can be more challenging than comforting after a while.

JOURNEY

To my daughters Denise and Monique, my son Dennis, and their spouses,

I am extremely proud of them. They are loving, caring, family oriented adult leaders in their fields; working unselfishly to aid and provide service to others every day.

In 2009 I was privileged to meet **our former First Lady Rosalynn Carter.** This opportunity came about while working for the St. Johns County Council on Aging and teaming up with Kurt Hubbard PhD(c) OTD, OTR/L Assistant Professor of the University of St. Augustine for Health Sciences as we were awarded a grant from the Johnson and Johnson Foundation and the Roslyn Carter Institute. The caregiver program I had been working on, was awarded a 2-year grant allowing us to carry out an evidence-based intervention for caregivers and their loved ones in their homes. This intervention helped make their dementia care experience both safe and empowering. Mrs. Carter's kindness, and sincere appreciation for the important role of caregiving, as well as the strategic role she has played in research and development of evidence-based interventions to help support the role of caregiving is monumental. Her work and dedication have helped millions of lives throughout the years. The Rosalynn Carter Institute for Caregivers is located in Americus, Georgia.

To learn more about The Rosalynn Carter Institute, her wonderful works, and legacy, you can go to their website: https://rosalynncarter.org/ or call: 229-928-1234

Last but not least, I give special thanks and recognition to Florida's St. Johns County Council on Aging and all of the wonderful and loving employees and volunteers whom I have had the honor of working with over the past 20 years. I came to this organization seeking information about what it would take to start my own Adult Day and Caregiver program as the one I had previously been working for was closing its doors for good. Much to my surprise, instead of advice, they welcomed me as well as our entire Day Care Program with open arms. I felt as if a miracle took place that day! I agreed to do the paperwork, and they agreed to provide a building. Within record time, our program was once again up and running, and all of my staff, participants, and their families were reunited once again. 20 years later, this program and our "Community Care-Giving Program continue to grow and serve many well-deserving families in our community. A few of whom you will have the opportunity to meet along our journey.

FORWARD

As a dementia care practitioner and educator, I have met some caregivers who were reluctant to learn the details about dementia. They expressed their fear that learning about what was to come would be too depressing. I can assure you, this book of guidance was not written to frighten or depress anyone called upon to accept the challenge, climb the mountain and forge the sometimes-rugged terrains of the dementia world. Rather this book is written to enlighten and empower you. To promote strength, courage, and support. To make your journey as positive, enjoyable, and rewarding as possible for both you and your loved one. It is my hope that throughout this journey you and your loved one form wonderful new memories together, from which you are able to internalize the rewards of a caregiving job well done.

This book is also written for others who may want to consider becoming an important part of a caregiving team - such as a family member, friend, volunteer, or hired caregiver. Your assistance, understanding, commitment, ability, and dependability to accept the challenge are monumental to both the caregiver and the care recipient. It is said that "You can't make a mountain out of a molehill". But perhaps with enough help, commitment, team training, and support, a team may be able to make a molehill out of that mountain! **With enough people sharing the load, the weight of the dementia world can feel much lighter, the path much smoother and enjoyable, and the experience more memorable and rewarding for all.** Internalize the feeling of reward within yourself for each assisting step that you take.

As you are well aware, no two people are alike. Each and every one of us sees the world through different eyes, perceives the world through different minds, and encounters different life experiences. Therefore, you may find that parts of this book may differ from some of the actions and experiences you are witnessing with the one you are caring for and your caregiving situation. You may find yourself at times disagreeing with some of the statements, views, ideas, and suggestions. Differences are to be expected and welcomed. They challenge us to be aware of our own uniqueness. The guidance I share is simply to be taken as such; and is not necessarily the only answer to the problem; or even the right answer for the one you and your loved one may be facing at any point in time. The guidance I share is what I have learned and experienced throughout my journeys. I pass this along to you in hopes that you can use what is helpful, leave the rest behind that is not. And be mindful of your own thoughts and ideas that can make your journey the best it can be.

Before beginning our virtual journey through the dementia world, it is important to take a close look at your life at this point in time. Are you able to let go, and leave behind the world you have been accustomed to? Do you have the strength and courage to venture out into an ever-changing dementia world? Some of you may already be very familiar with this world, yet find yourself caught up and lost at the crossroads. For others, you may feel this is not a new journey at all. You've gone through this before with another family member or loved one. Each person's background is different. Each journey is different. There is always something new to learn and experience with each person you care for. So, if you are ready to proceed on this caregiving journey with me, pack those experiences up, and bring them along! But remain open-minded to the ever-changing world of dementia! Just as no two people are alike; what worked for one may not work for another. As a matter of fact, what worked one day, may not work the next! That's one of the things that makes this journey such a challenging adventure!

JOURNEY

PREPARING FOR THE JOURNEY:

Before departing on this journey, have you gone through the steps to determine:

1. **Is this truly an untreatable illness your loved one is facing?**

When one shows signs of memory loss or confusion, it is important that they get a good physical exam.

Other Diseases or Disorders may mimic dementia, and it is important to rule them out:

      Depression

      Medication side effects

      Nutritional Imbalances

      Metabolic Disorders (Thyroid, hormonal, etc.)

      Infections

Poisonings

Brain Tumors

Usually Diagnosing Alzheimer's Disease or other related dementias involves a primary care physician specializing in this area or a neurologist.

Specialists can accurately diagnose 9 out of 10 Alzheimer's Disease cases through:

The Medical History and Information from the Caregiver

Physical & Neurological Exams

Ruling out: depression, side effects of medications, vitamin deficiency, thyroid problems, infections, strokes, tumors, etc.

They may perform one or more Memory Screening Test:(MMSE, MoCA, MINI-COG, Sweet 16)

They may order one or more Imaging tests:

(PET, CT, MRI)

They may Test for diagnostic & Statistical Mental Disorders (DSM-IV)

1) LEGAL ISSUES

It is very important for all of us to have a plan in place to determine who will be able to make decisions on our behalf if or when we are no longer capable of doing so. If your loved one does not have someone delegated already, it is important to determine this as early as possible to ensure your loved one is still able to participate in this decision-making on their own behalf. Advance directives for financial and estate management must be created while the person with dementia still has the "legal capacity" to make decisions on their own, meaning they can still understand the decisions and what they might mean. Otherwise, guardianship may be necessary.

Here are 2 websites where you can get information to help you plan:

www.nia.nih.gov/health/legal-and-financial-planning-people-Alzheimers

https://www.caringinfo.org/planning/advance-directives/

You may also be able to reach out to your local Agency on Aging, state legal aid offices, state bar associations, local nonprofit agencies, foundations, and social service agencies for information.

The list of legal issues below is long. All of this need not be completed before we begin our journey. Some of these things listed may not even apply to your situation; nor should you feel overwhelmed by all of it. Simply choose the things that are right for you, and make a "to-do" list for yourself. Take it one day at a time, as time permits. Check off the tasks you have completed as you accomplish them, and feel good about your accomplishments rather than overwhelmed. Try to relax, and remember the old saying:

"Rome wasn't built in a day."

A **durable power of attorney for health care** designates a person or an agent to make health care decisions when the person with dementia can no longer do so.

A **durable power of attorney for finances** designates someone to make financial decisions when the person with dementia can no longer do so. This document can help avoid court actions that may take away control of financial affairs.

A **Legal Guardian** may be necessary if your loved one is in a later stage of dementia and has not yet appointed a power of attorney. If they now lack the "legal capacity" or the ability to care for their own basic needs and are unable to designate someone to take care of their needs, it may be necessary to petition a court to appoint a legal guardian for them.

This is a costlier process and is another reason why planning ahead early is so beneficial.

A **living will** state a person's wishes for medical treatment near the end of life or if the person is permanently unconscious and cannot make decisions on their own about their treatment.

A **do not resuscitate order**, or DNR instructs health care professionals not to perform cardiopulmonary resuscitation (CPR) if a person's heart stops or if he or she stops breathing. A DNR can be obtained from and signed by a primary care doctor or Hospice and put in a person's medical chart. It is also helpful to keep an original yellow copy available to give to your loved one's local emergency room department.

Other things to consider:

1) **Who is managing your financial responsibilities and records?**

If your loved one with memory loss is the one who has been in charge of your household finances, now is the time to get involved or find someone else capable of handling these very important commitments and documents. How quickly this changeover of management occurs, is dependent on the current ability of your loved one, and their willingness to "retire" from these duties. If this task seems overwhelming to you, there are many organizations out there that may be of help to you including AARP (see link below) and others that specialize in this area.

https://www.aarp.org/money/investing/info-2016/affordable-financial-planning.html

Depending on your loved one's present capabilities, easing into the takeover of financial responsibilities may start out as a mentoring situation. This allows your loved one to train you or the designated person about how they manage bill payments, record keeping, and their filing system. Perhaps he/she still feels capable of continuing their present workload. In this case, convincing them how important it is to have a backup in case of an emergency, might be another way of having them mentor you and at the same time allow you to closely monitor their abilities. Little by little they may be willing to allow you or the new designee to assist or take over more and more responsibility as time goes on.

Some important things you may want your loved one to mentor you on:

Familiarity with their computer (if they are using one): Passwords; filing system

Financial information including:

Bank account & checking account information

Safety deposit box (if applicable)

Credit card statements & account numbers

Any outstanding Bills

Retirement funds

Loan Contracts

Mortgage Papers

Titles and deeds to property

Insurance policies

Tax information

Warranties

Other Legal documents:

Vehicle registrations

Wills. (name, location, and attorney holding it)

Living Will and other legal documents (give copies of advance directives to your loved one's physician and keep originals)

Social Security cards

Marriage license

Divorce papers (if applicable)

Military records (if applicable)

Cemetery plots, prepaid funeral expenses

There are many books on the market that can help you organize this. One such example is listed below:

The Household Financial Record Book: Create a user-friendly, hard copy listing of your financial assets for your spouse and heirs.

By Clark, T. Chris

Something else to consider:

(Elder Law Attorneys may be helpful in this area):

A **living trust** can avoid probate. It addresses the management of money and property while a person is alive. It provides instructions about the person's estate and appoints someone, called the trustee, to hold titles to property and money on the person's behalf. The trustee can pay bills or make other financial and property decisions when the person with dementia can no longer manage his or her affairs by using the instructions in the living trust.

JOURNEY

TRAIL MARKER 1
THE JOURNEY STARTS WITH ME (THE CAREGIVER)

It is an honor and privilege to join you today, on this caregiving journey. Allow me to be your guide, as we take a trip through the rugged and challenging terrain of caregiving. Together we will share some of the roughest yet adventurous, times of your life. Although this trip is not an easy one to take, together, we will strive to seek peace, contentment, and joy each and every step of the way.

So, let's get started…

There's a good chance you've already had some experience caring for a person in need of your help more than once in your life. Chances are great that you have quite a bit of experience in this field. Most people have experienced the responsibility of caring for another human being many times without giving it a second thought. For instance, you may have taken part in "child sitting" for someone else's child while their parents were away. Perhaps you have raised children of your own from infancy to adulthood. Perhaps you've had experience caring for a sick friend or parent after an accident, fall, or surgery. Chances are you had to set aside your own plans at one point in your life, to devote your time and energy to someone else. Despite encountering some challenges along the way, you were likely to discover that short term, caregiving was usually both manageable and very rewarding for both you and the one you were caring for. **Devoting time and energy to helping another in need can be the most rewarding act one can experience in life.**

However, if the demands for care increase and continue into long term, without assistance, those demands begin to outweigh one's time, energy and ability to provide the amount of care and patience needed to meet the demands of both yourself and the one you are committed to. Those humanitarian rewards of joy and accomplishment may start to dwindle.

As the workload builds, one is faced with the reality that the complexity of the situation requires a lot more time, strength, struggles, and sacrifice than one imagined when first taking on this challenge. One suddenly realizes their own limitations. This is not a single-person challenge. It now requires the work and support of a team. Caring for someone with a chronic illness such as a brain disease is most likely one of the most difficult challenges you will face in life. I can't emphasize enough, the importance of gathering a team to help you and

JOURNEY

your loved one through this journey. I can assure you, help is out there, and you will have time to gather it along the way.

It is normal for you to feel worried, anxious, perhaps even weak, or alone when faced with dementia care. When brain disease strikes a family member, it causes a domino effect on everyone near and dear to them. The caregiver's life suddenly changes unexpectedly. Being able to adjust and cope with this new way of life in the most positive way possible involves a lot of understanding and training. Therefore, if you find yourself feeling anxious and depressed, you have every right to feel that way along with a lot of other mixed emotions…

you are left to pick up the extra responsibilities that your loved one used to take care of. Don't wait too long to seek help to handle those extra tasks. It is important to be kind to yourself. Remember that you are only human. The caregiver who thinks they can manage both persons' responsibilities without help, is often the one who finds themselves angry, upset, short-tempered, and depressed. After all, you are only human. These negative feelings and actions often come from your inner self telling you "I'm tired, I need a break, I need help!!" Don't be afraid to seek that help

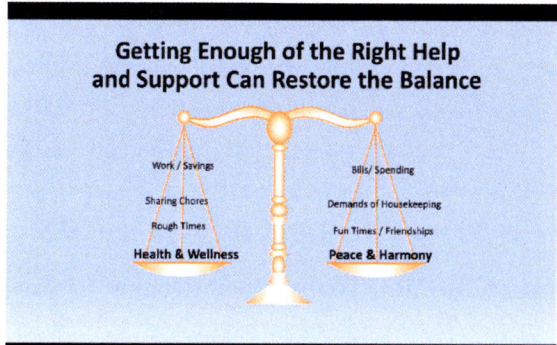

Brain disorders & Caregiving without help

Leads to Imbalance

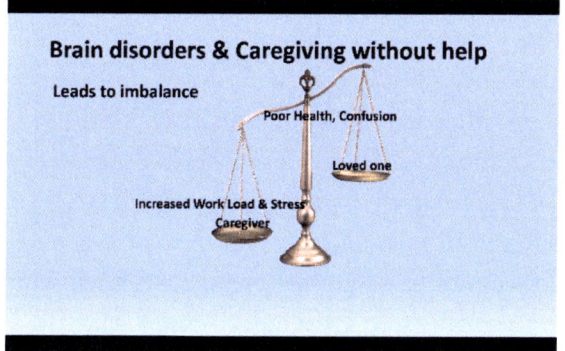

Caregiving is not something one usually plans for. Instead, one often finds themselves in a new situation, with changing and challenging responsibilities. You may find yourself in this new situation feeling mentally & physically unprepared – finding that you have little or no understanding of brain disorders and have little or no help to support you.

You may also find yourself experiencing negative feelings. When caring for someone with a chronic illness such as dementia. It is normal to feel upset, worried, depressed, and lost. It's also normal to feel guilty, abandoned and angry. Your life is drastically changing along with your loved ones. As this happens, expect to mourn for the loss of life as you once knew it. You are experiencing the loss of the strengths your loved one once had, loss of the role your loved one once managed, changes in your feelings about financial security, the loss or changes in future plans you once held. Because of all of this, you may find yourself experiencing different stages of grieving often referred to as anticipatory grief. Learning and practicing different ways of handling life changes will help you cope and get you through these unwanted feelings with the support of your caregiving team. Sometimes the grief you may be experiencing may trigger and cause you to relive thoughts of past losses and grief experiences. It is important to allow yourself to grieve. Share your feelings openly with someone you are comfortable with. Maintain hope while continuing to prepare for the inevitable end of life on earth. For those who find themselves stuck in a grief pattern, continuing to feel a lot of anger, guilt, and anxiety, a mental health professional may be of great benefit to you. Your physician or local Hospice organization may be able to connect you with this type of assistance.

The stages of caregiving grief as listed by the Alzheimer's Association, consist of denial, anger, guilt, sadness, and acceptance. These stages do not always happen in any specific order. You may move in and out of different stages throughout your journey. Our journey's final goal consists of reaching a place of understanding, acceptance, and empowerment to re-establish peace and harmony.

Let's take a closer look at some examples of these different **stages of grief** that you as a caregiver may experience:

<u>Denial</u> – Includes:

Hoping that the diagnosis was wrong – that your loved one is not ill

Expecting them to get better

Convincing yourself that your loved one has not changed

Attempting to normalize their problem behaviors

<u>Anger</u> - Includes:

Getting easily frustrated and upset with the one you are caring for

Feeling resentful about the demands of caregiving

Resenting family members who cannot or will not help

Feeling abandoned

<u>Guilt</u> – Includes:

Having unrealistic expectations of yourself

Feeling as though "I should have, could have…"

Feeling bad because you are still able to enjoy life while you feel your loved one is struggling

Feeling like you failed if things don't turn out the way you planned

Feeling bad if you find placement is necessary

Experiencing negative thoughts about your loved one

Wishing that he or she would go away or die

Regretting things about your relationship before the diagnosis

Sadness – Includes:

Experiencing frequent crying spells

Feeling overwhelmed by the losses you are facing

Hiding your emotions or displaying them more openly

Withdrawing from social activities or needing to connect more frequently with others

Acceptance – Includes:

Learning to live in the moment

Finding personal meaning in caring for someone who is ill Understanding how the grieving process affects your life

Appreciating the personal growth that comes from caregiving

Finding your sense of humor.

JOURNEY

Asking for and accepting help from others

Be assured, you are not alone. Experiencing these feelings does not mean you are a bad person. These feelings are a normal part of the grieving process.

Keeping those feelings and stress inside is unhealthy. One of the first important tools to pack for your caregiving journey is your ability to externalize!- It's not only o.k., but important to express your feelings – Not by screaming or yelling, but by verbalizing. Vent, Vent, Vent – & allow your loved one to do the same. If held inside, negative feelings can easily turn into poor health conditions. Therapeutic examples of ways to externalize consist of talking about it, crying, and being physically active. Find someone you feel comfortable talking to and talk about your feelings. Joining a Caregiver support group will also provide you with that opportunity. Not only will you be able to vent in your support group, but you will learn ways others have learned to deal and cope with difficulties. Take a walk, jog, or some other form of exercise. Don't forget to try meditation!

Ways to Cope:

Think about all of your feelings positive and negative.

Let yourself be as sad as you want, and accept feelings of guilt - they are normal. We will learn to work through anger and frustration, they are healthy emotions. Learning to catch these feelings early and discovering ways to let them out, away from your loved one, hold the key to self-control. It is also okay to feel love and anger at the same time!

Prepare to experience feelings of loss more than once. As dementia progresses, it is common to go through feelings of grief several times. Accept and acknowledge these feelings. No two people experience grief the same way. Some people need more time to grieve than others. Your experience will depend on how severe and for how long the changes have been happening in both of your lives, as well as the relationship you hold with each other.

Know that there are ways you can try to turn negative feelings around. – I learned and practiced this through the readings of Dr. Joe Dispenza. With some practice, you too can learn to take control of negative feelings (anger, anxiety, and many types of depression). As an example, if you find yourself getting angry when your loved one repeats and repeats and repeats… You can practice saying to yourself "I'm not going to let this anger me. I'm not going to let anger win. Instead, I'm going to look at this as an opportunity to problem-solve. I'm going to smile and respond with a positive answer or statement. Then I will try to break the repetition by singing his/her favorite song (or some other positive idea you may come up with).I am going to retrain my brain to view this repetition as a challenge that I can win. Instead of allowing it to anger me, I'm going to look at it as an opportunity to become a master of it and feel proud of myself for handling it in a positive way".

Dr, Joe Dispenza best-selling author of "Evolve Your Brain" writes: "You can choose to take hold of anger, anxiety, resentfulness, and depression and turn it around – by turning around the way you think".

As we move along, you will learn more about how to change the way you think in an effort to seek peace and harmony – You will learn about more ways you can "Retrain your Brain"

TRAIL MARKER #2
LEARNING TO ACCEPT –

Learning to Retrain Your Brain

The most helpful items we place in our backpacks will consist of the knowledge we gather and understanding about the challenges our loved one faces along the way. As we proceed on the journey, we will also learn survival techniques on how to deal with these challenges.

To better understand a little about what the person with dementia may be feeling and experiencing, it is helpful to look as far back as possible at our own earliest memories, our own life experiences. Close your eyes and take some time to recall memories as far back as you can. Reflect on your earliest childhood memories of the hardest, most frightening experiences you encountered at a very young age in your life. Try to recall the earliest memories of things that brought you anxiety and fear. As a young child were you ever lost, confused, or frightened by something? Were you ever not sure of where to go or what to do? What did it feel like to be frightened at such a very young age? What helped you feel better and safer again? Write this information down for future reference.

Now that you've given those experiences a lot of thought, close your eyes again and recall your earliest memories of things that made you extremely happy or excited in your early childhood. Perhaps it was a special birthday, holiday, or vacation. What were those feelings like when you were very young? What was your sense of time back then? If you were told your exciting day was coming up in a month or even a week; how long did that time seem to you?

Is there someone in your life that you consider or considered in your past to be your best friend? How did/does that person make you feel when you communicate over the phone, or share time together? How comfortable do you feel around a best friend?

A person encountering recent memory loss and confusion experiences a lot of anxiety. Since they are unable to recall what happened earlier that day, and are confused about what they are supposed to do next, they often feel lost. They seek security through their caregiver. When the caregiver is out of their sight, feelings of anxiety at being lost may occur. Remember how you felt as a child when you were lost, confused, and frightened? Remember what helped you get through it, and who or what relieved those stressful feelings? A key to helping a person with dementia find relief from the daily stress and anxiety that often accompanies those feelings of loss and confusion is to learn to better understand their feelings and build a dependable, comfortable, "best-friend" relationship with them. Best friends are dependable and provide comfort and support when needed most. Learning to provide "best friend" care helps develop the peace and harmony we are searching for and promotes feelings of happiness and security.

These long-term memories and experiences we recall in our own lives, help us to better understand the feelings a loved one may be experiencing in the dementia world. The more you can put yourself in the shoes of the one you care for, the easier it will be to understand their world and become that best friend.(Some of you may be fortunate enough to already be there).

Let's talk more about what "retraining your brain" is all about. It involves learning to change your vision of reality as you once knew it, as well as those expectations you've been holding on to. In some cases, it involves learning to lower your standards for the present and establishing a new way of thinking for this journey. Chances are this will not be a lifelong journey for you. You are welcome to go back to your old standards and expectations if you wish, after your caregiving journey has ended. But for now, we are entering a new world. When caring for a person with dementia it is important to try to put aside your reality for a while and understand the reality of the world of dementia. Brain disease often affects and obscures reality as we know it. There is a great chance that what the afflicted person perceives and experiences may be quite different from our perspective of reality. Trying to "fix" this obscurity, in an attempt to bring them back to our reality doesn't work. What their brain is telling them is very real to them. They are no longer able to get into our world of reality. It is, therefore, very important that we learn to try to understand theirs. We need to meet them where they are, validate and allow them as much freedom and control of their life as safely as possible. We need to allow them to communicate and express their thoughts and feelings in their own way.

Along with reality change, comes loss of abilities. For some, these losses are very gradual. Others may find them happening more quickly. These losses cause them to fail at the tasks they once may have been very proficient at. It is not unusual for a caregiver to become upset when the person you have been living with suddenly changes and stops holding up their part of their expected responsibilities. The person with dementia may often feel they have accomplished the task, but you may find this to be unacceptable. The same may hold true of a parent whom you may have always been able to come to for help, advice, and understanding. You suddenly find the tables are turned. It's no wonder you as a human being, get angry, upset, depressed. You may feel you don't have time for this. You have your own things in life to take care of. All of these feelings are normal. This is where retraining becomes so vital to caregiving. With enough understanding, help, and support, these feelings can be turned around. Your brain can be trained to a better way of thinking and feeling about this or any other difficult situation. Step by step, you will learn how this is done. Know that you are not alone. There are many of us out here to

JOURNEY

help support you through this journey. Caregiving does not mean you have to do this alone; nor should you. It takes a team. If you are having difficulty finding help, and friends or family ask "How can I help" – avoid turning their assistance away. Instead, have a list ready to present to them. If possible, have them pick a certain day of the week that they may be available to help, even if it is for only a few hours each week. This will provide you with a day to set your own appointments or fun activities. Retrain your brain to change from a feeling of not wanting to "bother anyone", to a feeling of providing others the opportunity to help someone. As mentioned at the beginning of our journey: **"Devoting time and energy to helping another in need can be the most rewarding act one can experience in life."** Allow your friends and family to experience this reward along with you. Some day they will look back and feel proud of their ability to assist.

Preparation for the caregiving journey involves learning what changes to expect, learning to accept them, learning to seek help, and learning to let go of previous expectations. For most, this doesn't happen overnight.

It is not uncommon for caregivers to feel nervous, anxious, angry, upset, and perhaps even frightened about the dementia world and the challenges it brings. To help overcome those feelings, let's look at what it takes for one to "Retrain Your Brain":

From early on, our brains have been trained to see life in stages of growth and accomplishment. We expect life to proceed in steps toward independence, success, and maturity. Dementia doesn't work that way. It changes things. When journeying into the dementia world, it is important for the caregiver to learn to change that old way of thinking, in order to reach the destination of peace and harmony.

Knowing what to expect in the dementia world makes a big difference in the way we think as a caregiver. A prime example of this is the birth of a child. One rarely gets anxious or upset to find that a newborn comes into the world incapable of doing anything for them self. A child is born confused about the world around them. They are unable to understand words or directions, feed themselves, bathe, walk, and are incontinent of bowel and bladder. In fact, without the assistance of another, this child would be unable to survive. Yet, we are not angry, shocked, discouraged, saddened, depressed, or frightened by these facts. Our brains have been trained to expect, accept, and prepare for this. We even celebrate the day we became a caregiver for that very helpless child, every year thereafter!

Our brains are also trained to expect life and abilities to proceed as the picture illustrates below:

One starts off as a helpless infant. In time, through assistance, experience, education, and support, those abilities change. The child becomes more and more independent. Until one day, he/she is ready to venture off into life on their own or perhaps with a partner they have met along life's way. If all goes well, one reaches their senior years, enjoys retirement, and lives "happily ever after" with family and friends.

Dementia changes that. It adds new steps in life which lead in the opposite direction. It takes a downhill turn. However, that does not mean that joy and happiness need to diminish with the loss of those abilities. Instead, we can train our brains to be prepared, to expect, accept, and find solutions for the difficulties, and rewards for accomplishments. **Retraining our brains help us focus on the bright side of every situation no matter what stage of life's journey one is in.**

When someone develops Alzheimer's disease and other related dementias, the slow progressive loss of brain functioning causes one's physical and cognitive **abilities** to age in reverse. I emphasize the word abilities because unlike the illustration, when one develops a dementing illness, the physical appearance of the body changes only slightly when compared to the changes it went through from infancy to adulthood. Other than wrinkling of the skin, a gradual loss of bone and muscle mass, and weakness, overall body appearance usually doesn't change much. Groomed appearance may change a little, as one may begin to pay less attention to their hair, make-up, shaving, etc.

The illustrations depict the aging and changes in abilities to help in the retraining process. They illustrate an understanding of the losses of functioning and comprehension one will encounter with Alzheimer's dementia. Little by little, one's abilities age in reverse. For safety reasons knowledge regarding lost ability is important to know and understand. This knowledge also provides us with the tools needed to set them up for success. When we see what our loved one is no longer capable of doing, and focus on the abilities they still have, we are better able to offer opportunities in their lives that they can still be successful at. For instance, meet Martha. Martha is no longer able to cook, as she is currently in a stage where her memory does not allow her to sequence. She no longer is able to comprehend cooking directions and often forgets that she left the stove on when finished with her cooking attempts. Martha's daughter is greatly aware of her mother's loss of cooking skills and instead, has provided her an opportunity to be successful with other tasks. She has given her the responsibilities of rolling dough, setting the table, and making simple sandwiches. She is still able to accomplish these tasks successfully. This increases her mother's feelings of helpfulness and increases her self-esteem. It is important that the caregiver be attuned to your loved one's current abilities, set them up with jobs they are interested in and can be successful at, then aid only as needed. Rather than focusing on what is lost, continue to focus on their remaining abilities and provide new opportunities that allow them to utilize existing skills.

Each step we take is meant to help fill your backpack with more and more understanding and support. Each path is taken to increase your knowledge and confidence in the important work you do, in an effort to promote ways of decreasing anxiety and replacing it with inner peace; as you specialize in and realize, the great job you are doing as a caregiver.

In a book titled "How to Say It to Seniors" "Closing the Communication Gap with our Elders" written by David Sole, MS, PA. the author depicts a clear understanding of the stages of maturity we all go through throughout life and the conflicts we face through each step. From his writing, we realize the struggles seniors face in their final years of life, and the important role others play in allowing them to work through their struggles. I have included excerpts from that book below:

David Sole refers to Eric Erikson's psychoanalysis on human development and the conflicts one faces and must get through in order to reach the next stage of life. If one isn't able to resolve the conflicts, they may get stuck in that stage and remain immature to society. Looking at a 2-year-old, the conflict they face is needing their mother yet wanting to separate from her to form their own identity. They often resist or throw tantrums as an expression of the difficulty they face resolving the conflict. It is best managed by giving them space, love, and guidance. Punishment is not recommended as it may delay the independence they are trying to obtain.

Teenagers face similar conflicts needing to separate from their parents while preserving their protection (such as a roof over their heads and financial assistance). When attempting to resolve their conflict they tend to either withdraw from their parents, lecture them, or engage in risky or identity-seeking behaviors.

Early adulthood experiences a conflict of new independence and the need to seek intimacy with others. This conflict is often referred to as an "identity crisis".

Middle adulthood faces conflicts of wanting to express strengths for personal gain, yet feeling a need to nurture others to contribute to society. They may also find themselves pulled in different directions raising children and taking care of one or both parents.

Seniors face a developmental conflict in the need to maintain control over their lives as it is constantly slipping away as they face many losses. This sometimes results in what we feel is "difficult behavior".(we will address this in more detail later on in our journey). Besides the need to maintain control, they face a need to discover their legacy that will live on after they are gone. Attempts to try and resolve the conflict of discovering their legacy sometimes produce what we sometimes refer to as "difficult communication" such as wandering off the subject, repeating stories, going off on tangents, describing something in endless detail, or postponing decision-making. Solie states "We can bridge this geriatric gap and facilitate their end-of-life tasks" if we stop fighting their attempts at self-control and allow seniors to manage their lives and tell their stories to shape their legacies. "Solie's writings may shed more insight into those stories of the past your loved one keeps repeating over and over. Perhaps it is their way of expressing their legacy. When you find the time, you may want to ask your loved one for even more details, and possibly record their words. The telling of those old stories may allow them the opportunity to fulfill their legacy.

There is no need to be fearful of or stress over the stages of dementia. Looking back at your own life once again, you've most likely experienced the sacrifices and trials of having to provide complete care to an infant; childproofed your home for a toddler; set limits and struggled with homework for the school-aged child, experienced the mood swings of puberty, and joys and anxieties of those dating years. It is possible you may even have had to play a part in college and/or career planning as well as financial assistance. Despite the hard times, you've probably found so much good in those days of raising the child, that most likely you wouldn't trade them for anything in the world.

Looking back at the experiences of raising a child, in a like manner, one can still find joy and happiness even when faced with the toughest and roughest of roads. You may one day look back at your caregiving struggles and feel the same. You are building new memories each and every day. Our goal is to make these memories ones you can be proud of.

As you the caregiver, slowly begin to retrain your brain to a new way of looking at and approaching caregiving, it is my hope as your guide, that this rugged path slowly becomes a little smoother and a more positive, and more rewarding experience than you thought possible. You may not like the road you are on right now, any more than your loved one likes what is happening to them. We are traveling this journey in an attempt to make things a little brighter for both of you.

Even with your best attempts at making things better as a caregiver, it is important to remember, our goal is not to make life perfect. Instead, we strive to make it the best it can be using the best of our abilities. I can't emphasize enough; how important it is for you to realize and feel good about the life-changing work you are doing. You are truly very special.

It takes time for one to retrain their brain to another way of thinking. Your loved one's abilities to uphold their roles in the household are changing before your eyes. This can be very frustrating and anxiety provoking. Especially to caregivers who expect things to stay the same. Unfortunately, dementia changes this. We too, must change our expectations of what that person is capable of doing now. To do this requires constant "retraining of our brain". Expectations need to be readjusted. This may take a while. After all, there's a good chance you may have been living with or at least know the one you are caring for, for 20, 30, or possibly even many more years. Your brain has held many expectations of the roles that person has played in your life. Retraining your brain takes time, but doing so brings more patience and understanding to accept and deal with dementia changes.

TRAIL MARKER #3: LEARNING TO LET GO...

    This virtual journey is being done on foot. – One step at a time. Get ready now, for a long and winding climb up the mountain of education, down through the bumpy stages of decline, and a hike through rugged terrains until at last, we find our destination place of peace and harmony. We are hiking with only a backpack and will continue to add contents to it as we go along. Therefore, there is no room for extra baggage. So, it is important to stop here and take a look in your backpack. Is there baggage that you have trouble letting go of? For those who have trouble **letting go of the past, the way things were before dementia struck,** know that you are not alone. This **is one of the hardest parts of the journey.** It's not easy to let go of your thoughts and feelings about how wonderful life was prior to dementia; how sharp, and vibrant, your loved one used to be; how much you were able to depend on one another. The great plans you shared about the rest of your life and how wonderful your future was going to be… And then it happened. Things began to change. It isn't fair. Why did this have to happen to me; to us; to **our** family?

Unfortunately, there is no room to drag along this type of weight on the journey. It will only make traveling more difficult. It will slow us down to a point of struggle rather than proceeding on into an ever-changing, challenging, and adventurous journey. Except for drawing on your own past experiences of what the world felt like to you as a child, in an effort to better understand the dementia world; **we will focus on the here and now. Once you are willing to let go of the past for a while and begin moving forward, there will be very little looking back at how life used to be.** Once you find yourself strong enough to **pack those old memories away** (time for reminiscing will come at a later date), you will be ready to travel forward through this journey with an open mind and some weight off your shoulders.

For those who feel you just can't let go of that baggage; you don't want your life to change; it was so wonderful the way it was; try this. Picture yourself and your loved one suddenly caught up in a huge tornado. Everything around you, your house, your belongings have all been destroyed. Fortunately, you and your family made it through. You are still alive, but your loved one was not so lucky. He/she was thrown through the air and developed a head injury, resulting in confusion and amnesia. You now struggle with the thoughts of what to do next.

This scenario may sound harsh. However, it should help you realize that dementia can sometimes have the same effect as that tornado on your family's life when it strikes. In order to get to the next step, it is helpful to realize that the lifestyle you once shared before is gone. Your life has drastically changed. In order to move forward, you must find a way to build up strength. It helps to stop looking back at what you once had and keep your mind open to what you have now. You are not alone. Others have experienced that same type of devastation. They too have been struck by these types of life-changing conditions. Little by little, along this journey, you will be introduced to friends who are here to help. They too, want to show you how it is possible to survive through this, and how to come out the other side feeling stronger. You will get a chance to hear their stories to help you make the very best of this very difficult situation you are facing. It may be hard to imagine now, but peace and contentment can be restored in your life once again. It takes a willingness to learn, a willingness to accept change, and a willingness to allow others to help you along the way and throughout your life.

Let's look at your psychological preparation. Are you feeling at peace with yourself and your present situation? Are you a patient person or do you find yourself uncomfortable with delays, in a hurry to get to the point or get things done, and easily upset? What is your level of fear and anxiety? If you feel more stress than peace most of the time, know that you are not alone. You are going through a lot of life changes which often have that same effect on others as well. This is where we stop, and take time to practice meditation. Getting into a habit of daily meditation helps train your mind to redirect thoughts away from stressors and replace those feelings with inner peace. It helps redirect you to the here and now. Meditation has been scientifically proven to be very beneficial for stress reduction. Meditation helps promote a more positive mood and an improved outlook on life. It can also be helpful in increasing your ability to sleep better and has been proven to help increase pain tolerance. If you are new to meditation: it involves concentrating on deep breathing exercises that help your body to truly relax and rid itself of uneasy feelings that often accompany stress. There are many CDs and other types of sound recordings you can purchase or get from your local library. YouTube also offers many free meditation recordings to choose from. I found that even a short, 5-minute meditation can be beneficial.

TRAIL MARKER # 4: LEARNING TO UNDERSTAND

Climbing a Mountain of Education & Enlightenment

There is a lot of educational material to cover on this journey. Thus, prepare yourself for a very long climb up to the top of "Mount Education". Our path starts at the foothills, where we take a look at some terminology:

Dementia – this term can be confusing. I often get asked, "What is the difference between Alzheimer's disease and dementia"? To simplify, I like to compare the term dementia to two words:

Sick – This is a broad term. When someone is told they are sick, they understand that something is wrong with their **body**.

It is no longer functioning as it should be. This can be caused by many known or unknown factors. Compare this term to the term dementia. **Dementia** describes a condition in which the **brain** is no longer functioning as it should be. It is showing signs of short-term memory loss as well as the malfunctioning of at least one other area of the brain. It too can be caused by many unknown factors.

Senile – Years ago, before Dr. Alzheimer performed his studies, as a person aged, most people who were able to live long enough, began to show signs of memory loss and confusion. Senility was accepted as a normal part of life and aging. Dr. Alzheimer's studies proved that memory loss and confusion were not caused by old age but rather a disease process. Not everyone who reaches their senior years becomes senile. The term dementia began being used as a more acceptable and clarifying term for someone with a brain disease experiencing short-term memory loss and impairment to other parts of the brain. Some physicians still refer to this, especially when it shows up in one's later years, as "senile dementia".

The world of science has come a long way. Researchers are getting closer and closer to finding the keys to help unlock the mysteries, slow down, and possibly even eliminate some of the diseases that may be causing the brain to malfunction in this manner.

Scientists are finding that there are many diseases that can cause memory loss, confusion, and other adverse effects on the brain. These diseases cause brain cells to malfunction and eventually cause death to the cells resulting in shrinkage of the brain itself. There still remains a lot of unknowns to be answered. For the sake of simplification and understanding, we will only be covering a brief explanation of some of the main diseases found to cause signs of dementia. Research shows that no matter what type of dementia one may encounter, once the brain has been compromised through one of these diseases, over time, disease spreading occurs throughout the brain resulting in similar brain function losses. Thus, the caregiving journey will require the same preparation and guidance to reach our pathways to inner peace and harmony regardless of the type of dementia your loved one may have. In fact, it is not uncommon for a person to have more than one type of dementia at the same time.

At this time, **Alzheimer's disease** is said to be the most common type of dementia. The cause of the disease itself remains unknown. It was discovered around 1906 and named after Dr. Alois Alzheimer in 1910. He was a German physician who graduated with a medical degree in 1887. He had a great interest in the human brain and commenced his education in psychiatry and neuropathology. He devoted much of his time to research caring for patients showing signs of senility. One patient in particular, Auguste Deter died at age 56. With his background as both a neuropathologist and a physician, Dr. Alzheimer was able to examine her brain under the microscope after her death. He discovered abnormal beta-amyloid plaques and neurofibrillary tangles. Thus, determining that senility is not a normal part of aging – but rather a disease process that causes memory loss, confusion, and loss of physical and mental abilities. This disease process is usually a slow, gradual decline. Progression can last 20 years or more, depending upon the person's other physical conditions. In **Early Onset Alzheimer's** however, – involving those showing signs and symptoms younger than age 65, the disease process may go much faster. Depending on a person's physical condition, life expectancy may be much shorter.

We're going to stop here for a moment, put down our gear, and have a bite to eat. I'd like to introduce you to Mrs. M. and her daughter Margaret. They live in a small cabin around the bend from here. Margaret makes her living by running a small refreshment stand next to her cabin, where she serves a variety of sandwiches, coffee, soft, drinks, and water to hikers in this area. This allows her an opportunity to make a small income while still being able to watch over her mother who is in the middle stages of Alzheimer's disease. Because of Mrs. M's loss of recent memory, as well as her loss of the concept of time, and loss of the ability to process what to do next, she gets separation anxiety if left alone. She feels the need to have her daughter in sight at all times. Fortunately, Margaret has a sister and two nieces who live in the area. Both nieces are in their 20s and take turns spending time with their aunt every weekend so that Margaret can enjoy time to herself or visit with her sister. Here we are now, I can see Margaret behind her stand. Mrs. M. looks content swinging on the porch swing nearby watching her. "Greetings ladies, how are things going for you? "From Margaret's comments, we learn that Mrs. M has been requiring a little more assistance from her. Therefore, she has increased her support system by adding a home care assistant to come in and help twice a week. Although caregiving needs have increased with Mrs. M's abilities declining, they have found that by adding another helper to their support team, they are still able to continue on and enjoy life in spite of it.

Lewy Body dementia (LBD) is the second most common type of dementia. Named after Dr. Frederic Lewy a Jewish German-born American Neurologist. In 1912, Dr. Lewy discovered abnormal protein deposits (alpha-synuclein) now known as Lewy bodies. These abnormal proteins create problems with thinking, behavior, mood, and movement. Caregivers are often times overwhelmed with behavioral changes that fluctuate with this illness. The sequence of stages in this type of dementia often differs from that of Alzheimer's. Recent memory as well as other cognitive abilities may remain intact much longer. Alpha-synuclein deposits are also indicators of Parkinson's disease as well as dementia. Early signs and symptoms of Lewy Body dementia include visual hallucinations, mood and behavior changes, movement disorders, and sleep disorders including acting out of one's dreams and fluctuating attention span. To learn more about Lewy Body Dementia would be to contact the LBDA, Lewy Body Dementia Association at: https://www.lbda.org/

Now, let's take a walk down this next path. I would like to introduce you to someone who has been diagnosed with LB. Here he comes now. "Greetings Lawrence. We are just passing through and thought we'd stop by to see how you are doing today."

"I was doing fine until all of these rabbits started getting in my way. They are all over the place. I've been trying to catch them, but they're too fast for me. Watch out, here comes another one. Move to the side, so you don't step on them".

"O.K. Lawrence, we're moving over and stepping aside. I can see your wife coming up the path looking for you, so we're going to move on. Have a great day".

As you learned previously, it is not unusual for people with LBD to experience hallucinations as well as mood swings. Trying to bring Lawrence back to reality by stating that there were no rabbits there, would have only made him angry. In the world of dementia what he is seeing is very real to him. Instead, we validated by telling him we were stepping aside. This showed him we were acknowledging his world and his request. If you also noticed, we kept a happy, positive temperament while doing so. People with dementia tend to mirror our behavior. If his experiencing a hallucination would have upset us, and if we had responded to him in an angry or anxious voice, there is a high likelihood his mood would have changed negatively as well. As long as the hallucination is not causing him any harm, we leave it alone.

If, however, the hallucinations affect his physical and mental well-being, such as feeling that bugs were crawling all over him, and he continued to scratch his skin and cause harm to his body, medical intervention may be necessary at that point to help minimize those hallucinations.

Vascular Dementia is caused by lack of adequate blood flow to a part of the brain possibly from narrowing and blockage of small vessels which may result in small mini-strokes, or sometimes a single larger stoke damaging and eventually killing brain cells. Symptoms can start with a rapid onset and then gradually change to a step-wise progression. A person may show a sudden decline in abilities followed by a long period with no change. Then suddenly they may have another drop in their abilities due to another bout of mini-strokes; then proceed again at that level for another long length of time without change. It is not unusual for someone to have this type of dementia along with another type at the same time (mixed dementia).

I would like to have you meet Veronica. She is one of the sweetest people I know in these parts. To look at her, you would never guess she has vascular dementia. She is still able to keep a clean house and care for herself. However, due to her short-term memory loss and some confusion, she has stopped driving and cooking. Her son Jason has come to live with her. He loves to cook, so it seems to be working out well so far. Here she comes now. "How are you doing Miss Veronica? It's always a pleasure to see you". "Why thank you. Same to you. "Where are you headed? "I'm not really sure. I thought I would take a walk to the refreshment stand, but I seemed to have lost my way."

"Does Jason know where you are? "I'm not sure of that either". "Well, we have some extra time, is it o.k. if we walk with you back home? Jason may be able to take you to that refreshment stand later". "Thank you, that will be fine. But how do you know my boyfriend, Jason? " "He's an old friend of mine. Well, here you are, safe and sound at home. I can see Jason in the window waving to you. It's been great talking to you".

It is not unusual for a person with dementia to get lost easily even in places they are familiar with. As the disease begins to affect their parietal lobes, they lose their ability to navigate. As it progresses further, they may require assistance with directions even to locate certain rooms in their own home. It is also not unusual for them to mistake the roles of family members after a while. As they lose more and more recent memory their thoughts are traveling back in time. Their most recent memory now comes from the long-term memories of years gone by. Depending on how much recent memory they have lost, determines where they are in time. In this case, it appears that Veronica does not even recall being married or having a son. She also feels a lot younger than she really is, as she sees herself back in time. Therefore, she knows Jason is a nice young man who came to help her out and live with her. Therefore, assumes he is her boyfriend.

A person with dementia does not always stay in the same stage all of the time. They tend to wean and wane slightly. For instance, when Veronica first wakes up, she may know Jason as her son and address him as so. However, toward evening, she may drift to another stage and once again see him as her boyfriend. Caregivers often feel saddened and depressed by the fact that their loved one does not recognize them. Know that, they may at times not remember your name or the role you play in their lives, but they do know that you are someone they trust, and who loves and cares about them. Together, you can still enjoy happy times together in spite of memory loss.

Frontal Temporal Dementia (FTD), consists of a group of diseases affecting the frontal and temporal lobes of the brain. It is one of the most common dementias that occurs under the age of 60. The fact that both Early Onset Alzheimer's and FTD strike at a much younger age than most dementias, they affect families in their prime. The spouse's dreams of a wonderful married life together become suddenly shattered. Often times they have young children who are also caught up in these serious life changes as they witness their parent going through this disease.

FTD usually affects one's personality. This form is known as the behavioral variant form. There are two language variant forms, one affecting the left side of the frontal lobe responsible for naming and pronunciation causing poor speech communication as well as reading and writing. The second type of language problem is the semantic variant in which the temporal lobes are involved where one loses the meaning of words. Loss of the ability to communicate properly often becomes very frustrating for them.

With these frequent mood changes, the young families' dynamics is often thrown in disarray. The unpredictable sporadic negative behaviors they become faced with may be more than they can handle, yet the cost of hired assistance or placement into a facility is beyond their financial means. If their loved on is a Veteran, the VA may be able to provide assistance. If they are not a veteran, the Department of Children and Family Services may be of help.

The caregiving spouse as well as the children in the family may benefit greatly from licensed mental health consolers often offered through one's job, school, medical insurance, or an anticipatory grief consoler through a local Hospice organization.

Behavior management can be very challenging especially when the person with FTD is exposed to more than one person at a time. Too much stimulation and too many people in their surroundings can cause them to become upset. Many people with FTD seem to do much better with a lot of 1:1 attention or in small familiar group settings. However, if they have a particular talent, they often do well at being able to share it with a group. They often feel more intelligent than others around them and take pride in being masters at a skill they may have. Sometimes allowing them the opportunity of showing off their skill to others, especially to those who enjoy their talent and give positive feedback boosts their pride and self-esteem.

Soon we will be stopping in to meet with Mr. Right. But before we get there, I would like to share a little information about him so that you can better understand his world as we enter it. He has been diagnosed with FTD and often has difficulty with anxiety when exposed to overstimulation and certain group activities. The activities that seem to upset him most are those in which more than one conversation is happening at a time in a room. Mr. Right is a bit of a perfectionist. He often feels that others around him are not performing up to his standards. He is often on a mission to make things right. This tends to make him very upset, either with the event or with the person he perceives is doing something the wrong way. Because of these feelings, his anxiety builds, and if left unchecked, can easily escalate into anger.

Although he has retained much of his vocabulary his speech is often incoherent. It is sometimes referred to as a word salad! And is a form of expressive aphasia. Most of the time he seems unaware of this problem. Communication for him is best received through body language and positive verbal feedback.

There he is now. He is standing near a group of teenagers over there that seem to be having a great time baiting their fishing hooks, fishing, and gathering wood for a campfire. Everyone seems happy except for Mr. Right. Let's go over and see what is going on.

As he sees and recognizes me, I can see that he is not happy with something the others are doing. "Mr. Right, I am so sorry, I can see you are upset. What can I help you with"? He replies while pointing at the boys baiting their hooks "No, is was worm wrong I they not fish told. And so mad told how." He begins shaking his hands and making fists as his anger mounts.

"Mr. Right, you have so much knowledge and experience with fishing. I'm so glad you're here. Let's go over here and sit under this shade tree. I want you to tell me all about your experiences with fishing so that I can pass it on to the others. They are young and inexperienced. I can really use your help and experience to teach others how it should be done". With these statements, you can see the anger and frustration Mr. Right once had, turn into pride and happiness. He suddenly felt someone in his world was on the same page, understood his frustrations, recognized his talents, took them seriously, and most of all cared very much about him.

Caregivers who learn to retrain their brains to see the world through the eyes of the person with dementia, soon discover that showing dignity and respect, building up self-esteem, and problem-solving go a long way to promoting peace. They learn to catch anxiety and frustration early, as it starts to smolder. This avoids it from escalating into anger. A friendly smile, a caring tone of voice, and positive body language are well-understood long after the language is gone.

Mrs. Right has just come by to take him home. I let her know what a great help he has been to all of us today. He smiles as he bids us goodbye. He is leaving a proud and happy man in spite of his FTD.

A person with frontotemporal dementia often remains oriented to time. Memory also remains intact in the early stages. It isn't until the later stages of the disease that symptoms including confusion and forgetfulness, and loss of motor skills arise. Eventually swallowing difficulties occur.

You can learn more about FTD by contacting the Association for Frontotemporal Degeneration

At https://www.theaftd.org/ or call their Helpline: 1-866-507-7222 or info@theaftd.org

Wernicke-Korsakoff Syndrome. These two disorders may occur independently or together. Often times they occur with chronic alcoholism due to thiamine deficiency (Vit. B1) which can damage the nerve cells. When this occurs, the person develops memory loss, learning and problem-solving abilities, and intellectual impairments. They may develop hallucinations, loss of muscle coordination, abnormal eye movements (back and forth), double vision, and eyelid drooping. Personality changes may occur. However, many of their other mental abilities may still be highly functioning.

Wernicke's encephalopathy causes damage in several parts of the brain, including the thalamus and hypothalamus. At this point, psychosis develops. Wernicke's encephalopathy represents the "acute" phase of the disorder and Korsakoff's represents the disorder progressing to a "chronic" or long-lasting stage. Here are 2 Resources to help you learn more about Alcoholism and Wernicke-Korsakoff syndrome:

https://www.caregiver.org/resource/wernicke-korsakoff-syndrome/

National Institute on Alcohol Abuse and Alcoholism (NIAAA)

Phone: 301-443-3860

Chronic Traumatic Encephalopathy (CTE) dementia – is believed to be caused by multiple head injuries resulting in concussions usually from contact sports like boxing and football. One's chances of developing dementia from these types of sports are believed to be nineteen times greater in one's 30s and '40s, and five- or six-times greater after age 50. in 1983 a CT (computerized tomography) scan of the boxer Muhammad Ali aged 41 at the time, showed evidence that his brain was slightly shrunken, and the fluid-filled ventricles enlarged. His physician at UCLA called it "dementia pugilistica." (A circular appraisal, Latin for dementia that happens as a result of being hit in the head.) Ali developed signs of neurological damage including tremors, balance problems, and speech impairment associated with Parkinson's Disease when he retired from boxing.

To learn more about CTE you can contact the CTE Society: https://www.ctesociety.org/

Normal Pressure Hydrocephalus – is a rare neurologic disorder in which excess cerebral spinal fluid (CSF) occurs in the ventricles of the brain with normal or slightly elevated CSF pressure. As the fluid builds up, it causes increased pressure around the surrounding brain tissue. This causes symptoms of walking abnormalities, dementia, and impaired bladder control. There are two types of NPH. The first type is idiopathic (iNPH). The cause is unknown but commonly occurs over the age of 60. The second type of NPH is known as a secondary form that can occur at any age. These types of dementia may be reversible through a surgically placed shunt from the brain to the abdomen to relieve pressure in the brain. Most people show significant improvement after shunt placement.

To learn more, you can contact the Hydrocephalus Association:

https://www.hydroassoc.org/about-normal-pressure-hydrocephalus/

According to a report by the National Institute on Health (NIH) in 2023, another type of dementia has been discovered, known as:

Limbic-predominant age-related TDP-43 encephalopathy (LATE). It shares similarities with Alzheimer's disease, causing problems with memory and cognition, and tends to affect people over the age of 80.

LATE was identified by researchers from autopsy studies. Their studies revealed abnormal clusters of a protein called TDP-43. This protein is involved in other brain disorders, including ALS (Lou Gehrig's Disease) and frontotemporal lobe dementia.

To learn more:

limbic-predominant age-related TDP-43 encephalopathy (LATE).

Rarer causes of dementia - There are many rarer diseases and conditions that can lead to dementia or dementia-like symptoms. Further information can be found at the National Institute of Neurologic Disorders. They include such disorders as Huntington's disease and Progressive Supranuclear Palsy.

Pseudo-dementias – some things such as severe depression, if left untreated, or unresponsive to treatment, can cause symptoms of dementia. The same is true of thyroid disease and thiamin deficiency. These are some of the reasons why it is so important for a person showing signs of early memory loss and/or confusion and other neurological deficits, to get a good medical and neurological evaluation as early as possible. As mentioned earlier, a good dementia workup should involve a history of the person's condition, Blood Tests (Thyroid, B1, chemistry, CBC), Cognitive testing, Imaging Studies, Psychological Tests, Depression assessment, and Neuropsychological testing.

Unfortunately, there are no known cures on the market today for those non-pseudo dementias. Researchers feel they are getting closer by studying the effects of newer medications that attempt to rid the brain of the accumulated beta-amyloid and/or tau proteins. To better understand the brain, the way it functions, and the medications used today to slow the progression of dementia, we will take the next steps forward.

Climbing upward on the Mountain of Education & Enlightenment

As we proceed up the mountain, we discover knowledge about how our brain works and what happens when a disease causes it to malfunction. Our ability to think, reason, react, and remember relies on the function of the brain and its main components - the neurons.

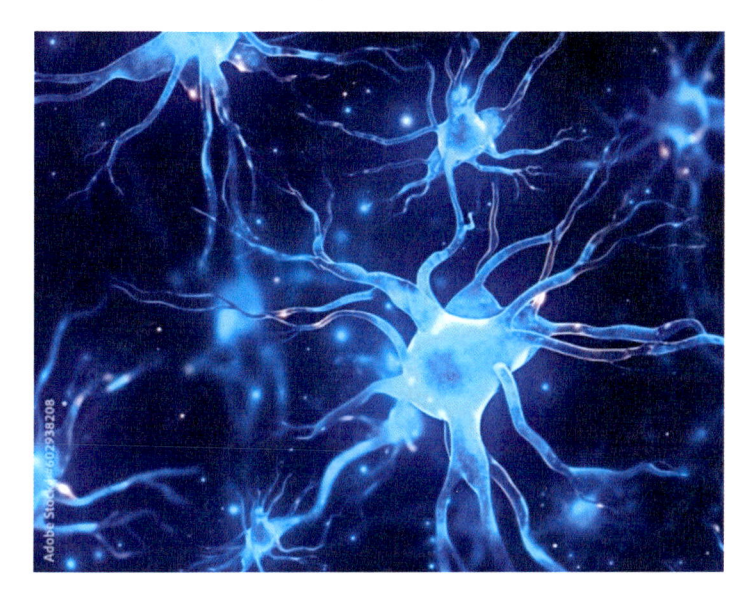

Since all of our abilities including movement, thoughts, reasoning, judgment, reaction, and memory rely on the brain, it is important to understand the basics. The human brain consists of trillions of very minute brain cells known as neurons. These cells are not attached to each other, but rather free-floating. Nutrients and information in the form of electrical impulses are carried from one cell to another on chemicals called neurotransmitters. Acetylcholine is one of the main chemicals (neurotransmitters) responsible for this information travel. It jumps from one cell and is picked up by the receptor site of another cell as it travels throughout the brain to its targeted destination. As one gets older, the amount of acetylcholine starts to decrease. In the case of most dementias, it is believed that even a greater amount of acetylcholine is lost.

The first type of Medication for Alzheimer's disease that was approved by the FDA was the cholinesterase inhibitors. There are 3 of them: Aricept (donepezil), Razadyne (galantamine) and Exelon (rivastigmine tartrate).Exelon may be used for Alzheimer's or Lewy Body dementia. These medications are given in an attempt to help improve the amount of acetylcholine in the brain in an effort to improve cognition. Not everyone shows signs of improvement after taking one of these medications. If improvement is seen, it is usually in the way of mild cognitive awareness and mild changes in the ability to function – such as being able to button a shirt when previously having much difficulty doing so.If one does see improvements, those improvements usually last only about one and a half years. After that, it is questionable if any further improvement will return. Side effects may be GI irritability, weight loss, anxiety, and sometimes wandering, pacing, shouting, or aggressive behaviors can occur.

The second type of FDA-approved medication that came on the market for dementia is Namenda (memantine).This medication is usually started in the middle stages of dementia and is used to treat moderate to severe dementia of the Alzheimer's type. It is taken in combination with one of the cholinesterase inhibitors listed above. It is an oral NMDA (N-methyl-D-aspartate) receptor antagonist. In other words, Memantine works by blocking the receptors in the brain that glutamate would normally bind to. This decreases the harmful effect of glutamate in the brain and may help improve symptoms of dementia. Too much glutamate leads to seizures and the death of brain cells. Too little glutamate can cause psychosis, coma, and death. It should be noted that urinary conditions that raise urine pH such as urinary tract infections, gastric suctioning that takes away stomach acids, kidney failure, and vomiting may decrease the urinary elimination of memantine resulting in increased blood levels of memantine in the system. Adverse side effects associated with memantine may include (but are not limited to) the following: fatigue, somnolence, headache, generalized pain, hypertension, constipation, and further vomiting.

Namzaric is a combination of memantine extended-release (Namenda) and donepezil (Aricept).

Just as with Aricept, Exelon, and Razadyne, if improvements from memantine or Namzaric are seen, those improvements usually last one and a half years. After that, improvements are questionable. None of these medications stop the disease. The neurons are still slowly dying. In other words: No matter how much "High Test" gasoline you put into a vehicle, if the engine is malfunctioning, even the highest-rated gasoline will not make it run any better. Most physicians are hesitant to take a patient off of these medications after that 1.5-year time period with the thought that if they do, there may be an even greater drop in abilities. At this point, it is not unusual for the physician to evaluate the patient's disease progression, then consult with the family to decide the length of time to continue or discontinue these medications.

Science is moving much faster today. Researchers are discovering ways of earlier detection through blood tests in which biomarkers for proteins: amyloid, tau, and alpha-synuclein may be able to be detected as well as neuroinflammation, and neuronal damage. Since late 2020, a blood test for Alzheimer's disease has been discovered and may soon be approved by the FDA and intended for adults 60 years old and older who show signs of dementia. It measures proteins linked to amyloid plaque buildup and the APOE4 gene variant. The prescription-only test is known as PrecivityAD.

They have also discovered skin tests for the alpha-synuclein protein as found in Parkinson's disease and Lewy Body dementia. Early detection is key to the newest disease-modifying drugs now on the market intended for those in the very early stage of Alzheimer's disease.

Aducanumab (Adulhelm) was approved by the FDA on June 7, 2021. Unlike the others, this medication works by decreasing amyloid-beta plaques in the brain. It is administered intravenously in monthly infusion doses. At this time, there is some controversy about the safety of this drug due to some trials showing side effects of brain swelling and bleeding. However, it may be a promising therapy for those in the early stage of Alzheimer's.

In January 2023, the US Food and Drug Administration (FDA) approved Lecanemab (Leqembi, Elsai). It is also a medication designed to decrease amyloid-beta plaques in the brains of those with **early-stage** Alzheimer's disease.

The trial showed modest cognitive benefit for patients with early AD- but at a cost of increased risk of edema or microscopic hemorrhages in the brain which occurred in 1 in 5 patients.

Treatment was given biweekly. After 18mos. It slowed cognitive decline by 27% compared to the placebo - 0.45-point difference on the CDR-SB (Clinical Dementia Rating scale).

So far, in 2023 it comes at a cost of approximately $26,500.00/yr.

A promising treatment being investigated at Brigham and Women's Hospital in Boston is a nasal vaccine that uses a substance called Protollin. It stimulates the immune system by activating white blood cells to migrate to the brain and trigger the clearance of beta-amyloid plaques. This exciting news seems to be very promising as Protollin has been found to be safe in other vaccines.

We've learned a little about the minute brain cells, the neurons as well as medications and the latest research. Now, let's look at the larger picture – the lobes and inner parts of the brain, and how they function both normally and when diseased.

Although you will be hearing and seeing a lot of medical terms including names of parts of the brain, do not feel it is important to know and memorize them. **The most important takeaway from this climb is in being aware of what happens when the brain is diseased and malfunctions. This gives better insight as to the changes in behavior, losses of understanding, and losses of abilities you may be seeing in your loved one.** Being exposed to this mountainous information helps the caregiver develop more patience and understanding as changes occur.

Limbic system

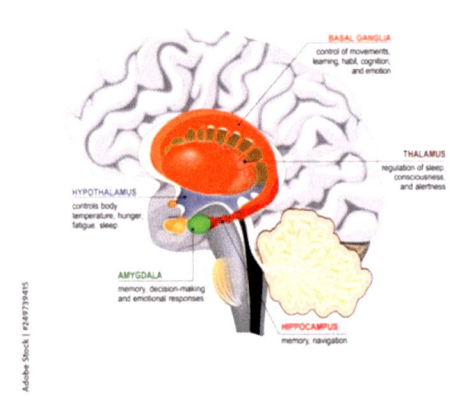

We shall start with the part of the brain that is most noticeably affected when a person develops Alzheimer's disease and other related dementias (ADORD). The part I am referring to looks somewhat like a microphone and is located in the temporal lobe of the brain. It is known as **the Hippocampus**, a part of the Limbic System as seen to the right of the diagram above. The hippocampus is responsible **for short-term memory**. It picks up current information from your 5 senses (sight, smell, hearing, taste, and touch) as you subconsciously decide how important the information is and how much of it you want to retrieve. For instance, if you feel the information, I am sharing with you today is not pertinent or is boring to you, your hippocampus may be ignoring most of the input it is receiving from you (similar to daydreaming during a lecture). You may find your recall of this information at a later date to be sketchy. On the other hand, if you found the information interesting and pertinent, even if you were unable to recall the information word for word, you would recall enough information at a later date, to realize you've heard about this before. This might allow you the opportunity to return to this mountain, or other sources of research, in an effort to locate the details. The same is true of all of your experiences throughout the day. For instance, the time you woke up today, what you had for breakfast, and what you did in the last hour. All of these things are stored in your hippocampus.

When a person develops ADORD (Alzheimer's disease and other related dementias) the hippocampus is one of the first noticeable areas to be affected. When this area of the brain becomes diseased, it is no longer able to do its job and hold on to new information. Knowing this helps the caregiver understand why their loved one keeps asking the same questions or keeps telling the same story over and over again. Their brain does not remember that they've already asked or told you that before. It is also important to understand that when this area is diseased, instructions given to your loved one with dementia are literally going in one ear and out the other. The hippocampus is not able to store it. For example, if you are out in public with your loved one and suddenly have to leave their side for a few minutes, and you say to them: "Sit here and don't move, I'll be right back"; no sooner will you step away, that the information and instructions you've just given them will be gone. Therefore, the person you have just instructed, despite your best attempts to keep them safe and secure, will most likely get up, be worried and anxious, may be thinking "Where am I? How did I get here?" and wander away looking for you or something familiar. It's not that they are trying to disobey your request or are being deceitful, it's just that they have no recollection of the previous instructions or explanation. For a while, giving them written information can be helpful. However, as the disease progresses, even the written words will lose their meaning. One of the caregivers' main jobs is to constantly assess the person's understanding and abilities so as to keep things safe and secure.

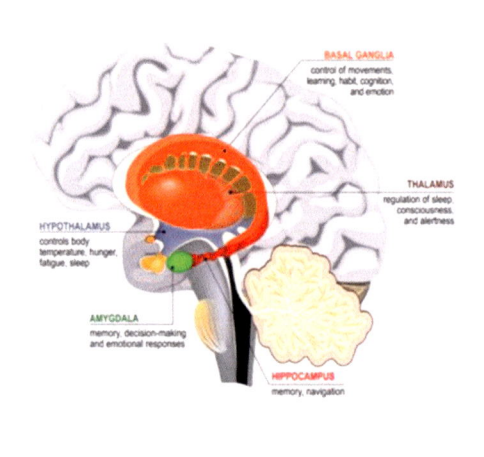

As the disease progresses, the hippocampus loses more and more recent life memories. Therefore, recall is limited to older and older long-term memories. **The longer the disease progresses, the farther back in time those recalled memories go. The old memories become as vivid as if they just happened yesterday.** The person's thoughts and abilities are aging in reverse. This explains why a person may eventually perceive their spouse as their father or mother. They know that the person they are living with is someone who loves them. However, they may no longer remember ever getting married.

They feel they are back in time and much younger than they really are since their memories are telling them so. Therefore, the spouse may now be perceived as an "older person" who loves them and is living with them. They start to believe the spouse must be their father or their mother. The same holds true of an adult child. Eventually, the son if living and caring for his mother in the home, as you saw previously with Veronica, may be perceived as her boyfriend. She may not recall ever being married or having children and knows that the man living with her cares about her very much. Therefore, begins to perceive him as her boyfriend or husband. It is not unusual for a 90-year-old person with dementia to tell someone that their mother (who has been dead for several years), is coming over for dinner. Trying to orient the person with dementia to the present is not advised. After all, these thoughts are very real to them. That person's recollection of just being in contact with their parent is very vivid to them. Therefore, telling them that their mother is dead will either make them feel the loss as if they were just hearing it for the first time, or make them feel extremely anxious because "No one believes me. I just saw my mother and I have to get ready for her dinner visit." Instead of trying to use orientation, we use validation. It is important for the caregiver to try to get into the dementia world since they are no longer able to get into our reality. Therefore, we approach this with the thought that the person with dementia is always right. Rather than butting heads trying to correct them, we learn to "go with the flow". Validating helps by sending the message, "I understand your feelings". So, if they feel their mother is coming over for dinner, an example of a response might be, "You and your mother have always been so close. Tell me more about your favorite times with her". This type of response does not confirm that her mother is still alive, yet validates the happy feelings she might have about her mother and may help distract her from the idea of her arrival for dinner. If she still insists on setting a plate for her, it is wise to let her do so. Avoid butting heads, "Go with the flow". When mother doesn't show you may be able to convince your loved one that mother thought you meant next week! More on this subject will be discussed later.

Another area of the brain, called the **Amygdala (fight or flight area** in green) is located at the lower end of the hippocampus. This area of the brain is usually **able to retain recent information involving high emotions much longer** than the hippocampus. An example of this might be a fire in the home. If a person with dementia was suddenly faced with the anxiety of being in a house fire, there is a great chance that their amygdala will recall that incident over and over again. The same may hold true of an event they are very excited about. For instance, plans to go to their favorite place of interest. They may ask the caregiver over and over throughout the day or even throughout the week if it is time to go yet. This often confuses caregivers who are unaware of the brain's physiology. It may appear to them that their loved one may have a better recollection than they admit to, and some may even begin to feel that their loved one may be faking their disease, as they can remember this, but are unable to recall so many other things. Knowing about the Amygdala, helps a caregiver better understand why this change in recall. It is also helpful to warn the caregiver not to share too much high-emotional information with your loved one too soon if you want to avoid being asked about it a million times before the actual event!

Also located in the temporal lobe is the **hypothalamus. This area controls body temperature, hunger, thirst, and some behaviors including sexual behaviors, fatigue, sleep, and circadian rhythms.** When this area is diseased, people get cold very easily in temperatures where others are very comfortable. It is not unusual for a person with dementia to want a sweater or blanket on in air-conditioned rooms. They also need to be monitored closely in the summer sun as they are also prone to heat stroke and should be kept well hydrated. Hydration can become a challenge as the malfunctioning hypothalamus may no longer tell them they are thirsty. For some, although rare, it may work the opposite. They may feel thirsty all the time and actually overhydrate. The same holds true with appetite. Some people feel hungry all the time, do not recall eating, and after completing a three-course meal, be heard to say "I'm starving, I haven't eaten anything all day! "For others, they may lose their appetite and refuse to eat most meals. In the final stages of Alzheimer's disease, all will develop what is often referred to as Alzheimer's anorexia. In this "Failure to Thrive" stage they no longer feel hungry, often have much difficulty swallowing, and weight loss is inevitable. Therefore, physicians are not concerned if, in the early stages of the disease, one gains a little weight as that will diminish in the end.

For those without an appetite, liquid supplements are usually recommended. Unless there is a GI or swallowing problem in the early stages of the disease, tube feedings are not recommended in the middle and late stages. The reason for this lies in the fact that in the last stage of the disease, people with dementia often lose most of their ability to swallow. In the case of tube feedings, there is a good chance the person will aspirate and not recover. Comparing the two options, it is believed that a person in the end stage of dementia no longer feels hungry or thirsty. It is the body's way of shutting down. It is also important at this time, to state that not everyone gets to the last stage of the disease.

For some, other fatal medical conditions may occur unrelated to dementia, such as severe pneumonia, heart or kidney disease, a massive stroke, or the inability to recover from breaking a major bone.

Fatigue, sleep, and circadian rhythms are also affected when the hypothalamus is diseased. Some people are up most of the night and want to sleep during the day. This presents a big challenge to caregivers as their sleep is also interrupted. This can drain one's mental abilities and put their physical health at real risk. Some people with dementia benefit from plenty of daytime exercise, fresh air, and supplements such as chamomile tea and or melatonin at night. Others may require mild sleep medications. When all else fails, if able, taking a daytime nap as your loved naps or another person watches over them, may be of benefit to the caregiver to ensure proper rest.

A diseased hypothalamus may also result in over-sexual behaviors. The person may feel as if they were back in their teens or young adulthood once again and often become overly stimulated. This may be a big challenge for a caregiving spouse. Some feel too embarrassed to mention this to the physician.

However, if this problem exists, there are treatments available. It is important to mention the problem to the doctor. Sometimes behavior management can help curb this. Also, the physician can take a look at the medications the person is currently on, as some medications also have this side effect. If that is not the case, there are medications on the market that can help to decrease libido.

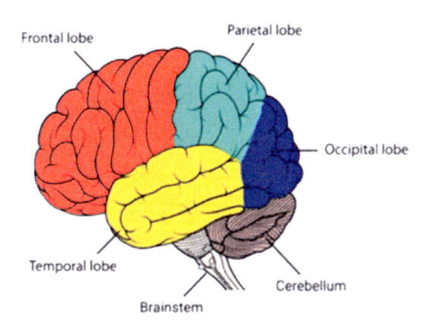

[Diagram of brain showing Frontal lobe, Parietal lobe, Occipital lobe, Temporal lobe, Cerebellum, and Brainstem]

Moving on to the **parietal lobe**, this area interprets sensory information. It is responsible for the **sense of touch and limb position**. It makes us aware of where our limbs are located and **tells us where we are in space and time**. If damage occurs to the right side of the parietal lobe, the person may become unaware of and neglect the limbs of at least one side of the body. They may lose the ability to write or draw things. A person whose parietal lobe is diseased may reach for a glass and miss it altogether because they were unaware of where the hand is located with respect to the glass. Damage to this area also interferes with the understanding of where one is in space. It is not uncommon for a person in the later stages of the illness to get lost in their own home even if they have been living in the house for several years. They may wake up at night and start opening closet doors in an effort to find the bathroom. Their brain loses its ability to navigate. Damage to the front part of the parietal lobe on one side causes numbness and impairs sensation on the opposite side of the body. The person may also have difficulty identifying sensations such as heat, cold, or pain. The time concept gets distorted. They may wake up after a late nap, and think that it is morning all over again.

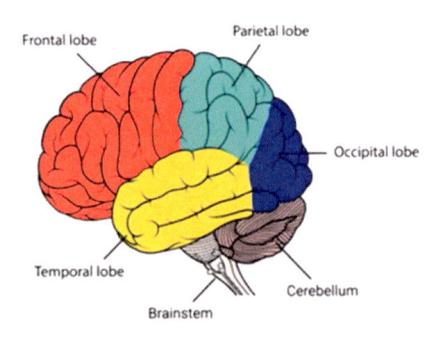

The frontal lobe is sometimes referred to as the "Master Mind" of the brain. It is involved in reasoning, judgment, motor control, emotion, and language. A person whose frontal lobe becomes damaged tends to lose their "filters" of what is socially appropriate. It is not uncommon for someone whose frontal lobe is damaged to display inappropriate behaviors such as undressing in public, or saying the first thing that comes to their mind regardless of how it may negatively affect the one they are speaking to. The frontal lobe also contains the motor cortex, which is involved in planning and coordinating movement. The prefrontal cortex is responsible for higher-level cognitive functioning. Another area of the frontal lobe known as Broca's area, is responsible for language production. With Alzheimer's disease, language is lost gradually. When one first loses words, they begin to describe. An example might be a conversation about a picture on a wall when the person begins to say "I like that – um- that wood around the picture". If they are unable to recall the word frame, they may attempt to describe it. This type of loss of words is known as expressive aphasia. Throughout the disease, more and more words become lost. As this worsens, they begin to develop what is known as receptive aphasia. They are no longer able to make sense of the words spoken to them. If they spoke more than one language in the past, and English was their second language, as the disease progresses, they will usually revert back to the language they spoke as a child. Often times they mix the languages together, and eventually, even their primary language becomes uninterpretable. At this point, the use of body language and positive facial and voice tones become our major way of communicating. Try humming a familiar song instead of speaking the words and see if someone can guess what you are trying to communicate. Or, try watching a TV program without the sound. See how much you are able to understand what is being communicated and what is going on. Body language including facial expressions plays a big role in communication and response.

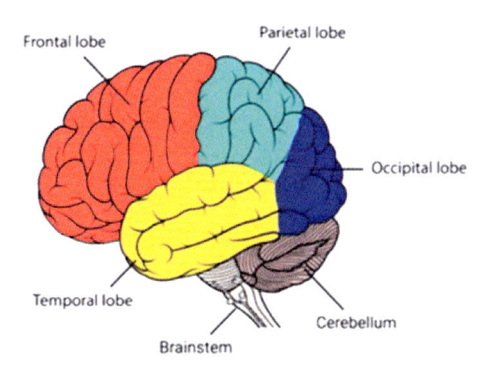

The next area of the brain to discuss is the **occipital lobe** located in the back of the brain. Fortunately, most of this area is not affected by Alzheimer's or related dementias. This area is **responsible for the vision and making sense of what one sees.** Fortunately, one does not go blind from the dementias. However, there is an area at the upper tip of the Occipital lobe that does become affected. Several things begin to happen with your loved one's vision.

There is a **loss of peripheral vision.** If you approach a person in the middle and late stages of dementia quietly from behind, they usually become startled due to loss of peripheral vision. Loss of this site also presents a safety issue as one may attempt to sit down on a chair (especially one with no arms) and miss the center, falling directly to the floor. For this reason, it is a good idea to keep a close eye on someone in this stage as they attempt to get in and out of chairs. Grab bars next to toilets and shower chairs are also very helpful.

Another vision change is a **loss of being able to see in 3 dimensions.** When loss of the ability to see in 3 dimensions occurs, steps, curbs, and uneven ground becomes hazardous. You may see a person walk with a shuffle while on uneven ground. They tend to drag their feet or step forward several times with one foot to help them determine if the ground is flat and safe to walk on in front of them. With the loss of 3D, it is extremely difficult to see where the steps start and stop. It is important for someone to be in front of and guide a person down a flight of steps. Otherwise, they may think they are at the bottom, step out in mid-air, fall to the ground, and fracture a hip. When one does not see in 3D, dark areas on the floor may also be perceived as holes. Therefore, it is not unusual for the person to try to step over the black rug or tile in an effort to avoid falling into the hole!

A person may also experience what is often called "mind-blindness". **"Mind-blindness" usually occurs in the later stage.** At this point, **the person sees an object, but the mind is no longer telling them what the object is used for.** An example of this would be a person with dementia picking up a fork and combing their hair with it. They may pick up a knife and try to eat their food with it. At this point, it is best to give the person only one utensil at mealtime rather than 3 or more. To help promote independence, finger foods such as sandwiches prove to be very helpful and less confusing. The pincher reflexes of the fingers remain intact for quite a while.

The Cerebellum, located below the occipital lobe adjacent to the brain stem is responsible for muscle control, regulation of movement including coordination of walking, posture and balance. Damage to this area results in unsteady gait and posture changes. They may develop a lean which can be toward the right, left, forward, or backward. Over time, damage to this area can result in the person to lose their ability to walk or to hold their head up for any great length of time. Language processing and some cognitive changes may also result when this area is affected.

TRAIL MARKER # 5
DESCENDING DOWN THE MOUNTAIN –

Through the Stages

We've finally made it to the top of Mount Education, and now have a long adventurous way to go back down. On the descent, we find ourselves ready to explore the stages of the dementia world. The education gained so far, has led us to a better understanding, and helps re-train the brain from the world we once knew to a world changed by brain disease. Retraining involves acceptance, which leads to empowerment, where we hope to find the peace and harmony we are searching for.

During our climb upward, we've reviewed the brain and how it works. We've learned what to expect when it malfunctions due to a dementing illness. As we move downward and forward, we will be encountering the stages of dementia and changes that arise with each stage. With the knowledge gained so far, these changes should make more sense to you. Reflecting back, you learned that in Alzheimer's disease abilities are usually lost in the reverse order from which they were gained. Not every type of dementia follows this exact same order of loss. Therefore, staging for Alzheimer's disease may differ from someone with one of the other related disorders. Nonetheless, with most types of dementia, once the brain has been compromised by a dementing illness, it usually spreads to other parts. Hence, although the order of stages may be different for your loved one with Lewy Body or Frontal Temporal Lobe dementias, eventually similar losses may occur in a slightly different order. Also, not everyone with dementia reaches all stages. Just as it is uncertain how long any of our lives will be – due to accidents, injuries, or unexpected health changes that may occur, the same holds true of someone with dementia.

As we pass through each stage along the way, you will be introduced to caregivers who have taken this journey and whose loved one is currently in that particular stage. This will give you a "birds' eye view" of how brain retraining has been helping them manage and provide care in a way that promotes positive effects on their lives and the lives of their loved ones. Although many admit, it is not always easy, they have learned ways to deal with the hard times and attest to have once again regained peace and harmony in their lives.

There are several ways to stage Alzheimer's and other related disorders. They follow the same course, but some staging methods have more levels. Some go into more detail than others. Many physicians today use the simpler method of staging and refer to the stages as Early, Middle, and Late-stage **dementia.**

One of the most detailed ways of staging was developed by a group of psychiatrists led by **Dr. Barry Reisberg, MD. Professor of Psychiatry at NYU Langone Health.**

(You can learn more about him and his great works by going to med.nyu.edu/faculty/barry-reisberg)

Dr. Reisberg was **one of the first to describe the important symptoms of Alzheimer's disease and its clinical course.** His staging tool known as the **Global Deterioration Scale** is still used worldwide today. **It gives an overview of 7 stages.** After studying people closely with Alzheimer's disease throughout their clinical course, he determined that their symptoms followed a similar pattern as their Alzheimer's disease progressed. It also became clear, that the person's abilities did not remain constant throughout the day. Instead, they tended to wean and wain back and forth, perhaps related to the increased energy or lack of energy in the brain at any given time.

This is a brief explanation of each of his stages. In addition, I will be introducing you to people who are experiencing some of these stages.

The scale starts with:

Stage 1 as being a normal brain – with no sign of dementia, as it is felt one likely starts with from birth.

Stage 2 describes Normal Aging Forgetfulness. It refers to a normal brain that is either aging or the person is multitasking (not concentrating on what they are doing).Chances are you've experienced this yourself at times when walking into a room and suddenly wondering "What did I come in here for? "After leaving the room, the reason usually comes back. This is considered normal forgetfulness and is not a sign of dementia if the information is later recalled.

In Stage 3, also known as Mild Cognitive Impairment (MCI), a person may noticeably start to repeat. Their capacity to perform complex functions becomes compromised. Job performance may decline. This is usually a sign of Early Alzheimer's disease. However, in some cases, the progression may stop here.

Meet Mrs. Jones. Her husband has currently been diagnosed. She was told he has Mild Cognitive Impairment. Mrs. Jones used to get very upset with her husband when he would repeat the same questions over and over. She became very angry and tired of answering him. She also became very upset with him when he began missing bill payments or overpaying others. When asked about it, he would deny that he made a mistake, or that it was his fault. She began receiving guidance through her care-giving journey several months ago and hence has learned to retrain her brain. She has learned that the part of Mr. Jones's brain that holds onto new information (his hippocampus) is compromised. Because of this, his repeating, missing a payment, or writing two checks for the same payment; is due to his lack of short-term recall. He is not aware he has done any of these things. Mrs. Jones's brain has been retrained to understand and expect these situations to occur in the world of dementia. Therefore, she has learned to expect, accept and answer those same repeated questions as though it were for the very first time. She also tries to let him continue the conversation by returning his question with "I'm not sure, what do you think about it? "If the repetition continues, she may sometimes try to change the subject. If that does not work, she uses the phrase, "Hold that thought, I'll be right back", and leaves the room for a short while until he forgets about the question! Using any of these skills helps avoid frustration and anger for both of them. She has also learned to take the time to work with her husband on bill paying; plans to set up an automatic bill paying with him through their bank, and realizes the time has come when she needs to closely monitor and learn the family money management. Knowing and accepting this, she feels empowered to keep moving forward with their life and find solutions to each problem as it arises so that peace and harmony prevail. In spite of his MCI, they continue to go out to dinner with friends, and enjoy fishing and taking walks in the park together.

Stage 4: Mild Alzheimer's disease. Diagnosis can be made with considerable accuracy in this stage. Loss of short-term memory is very obvious. Deficits include decreased ability to manage finances and prepare meals for guests, shopping may become more difficult. They have difficulty writing the correct date and the right amount on the check. Supervision and assistance are usually needed in these areas. Mood changes such as a flattening of affect and withdrawal may occur.

Meet Mr. Smith. His wife fluctuates from Stage 3 in the morning to Stage 4 in the evening hours (Sundowning).Mrs. Smith starts off each morning by putting on the clothes he has laid out for her, then coming to the breakfast table. She asks her husband the same question every morning "Who bought the lovely flowers"? She is referring to the same waxed floral arrangement he purchased for her last year that sits in the middle of their table. "I did my dear. I thought they would brighten up your day, as you brighten up mine every morning. "Rather than getting upset with that same question every morning, he has turned it around and learned to use it to set the stage for a positive start to their day. Mrs. Smith is unable to cook. Not long ago she attempted to do so, forgot that she had started the meal, and walked away from the stove, burning the food.Mr. Smith has learned to do all of the cooking now but chooses to take her out to dinner several times per week as a treat for both of them. He likes to take her out early to avoid large dinner crowds which often make her uncomfortable, and prefers to get back home early before the possibility of Sundowning may occur. Evening time is more confusing for Mrs. Smith. She is no longer able to change her clothing. Taking off and putting on her pajamas involves too many steps for her affected brain to carry out. These things used to upset Mr. Smith. He once felt depressed over the fact that his beautiful wife whom he depended on for so long to make him delicious meals and shop for all of their clothing and grocery needs, was now dependent on him for doing all of these things. He has re-trained his brain to look at the situation in a new light. He now finds joy in the fact that he is able to be so helpful to his wife who is now in need of his assistance. He has learned not to dwell on what used to be but instead focus on the present. His focus is on what his wife is still capable of doing, and what makes her happy. His anger and depression have now turned to feelings of fulfillment as he reaps the rewards of helping his wife in need. He has also learned to accept help from their grown children. Although they may be busy with lives of their own, spending time with their mother, allows them to reap some of those positive rewards of giving and receiving as well.

Stage 5: Moderate Alzheimer's disease. At this stage, it is unsafe for the person to be living alone. Assistance is needed in providing adequate safety and food, as well as assuring that the rent and utilities are paid and the finances are taken care of.

Meet Mr. and Mrs. Dee. Mrs. Dee's mother although in her 50's has been showing signs of forgetfulness and confusion. After being examined by her MD and neurologist, it was determined she had early-onset Alzheimer's disease. She had been living alone in her own home for several years, and although it was obvious, she was not able to maintain it inside or out, she refused to leave. In fact, she was refusing help altogether from anyone, including her daughter. Mr. & Mrs. Dee were torn over what to do at this point. This situation appeared as a fork in the road. Removing her from her unhealthy home and lifestyle against her will would cause great trauma and torment to her already confused world. However, leaving her in this type of situation was both unhealthy and dangerous. This situation proved to be very traumatic for her daughter and son-in-law. At this point of their journey, they found their terrain to be very rough. Once a loved one reaches stages 5 and 6, it is no longer safe for them to live alone. Yet, for most people, their home is their comfort zone. Like Mrs. Dee's mother, they may also be uncomfortable allowing others to move in with them. Mrs. Dee found her caregiver support group to be very helpful in guiding her through this tough time. Step by step, she worked at trying to gain her mother's trust while allowing her mother to maintain control of her own life. Her daughter's patience paid off as she slowly gained that trust. Little by little, her mother would accept her daughter's help. At first, she allowed her in the house, where previously she refused to do so for fear that her belongings would be disturbed (as she was a hoarder).Once inside, she slowly allowed her to wash a few dishes. Little by little, Mrs. Dee would open the refrigerator and cupboards to see how much food her mother had available. This journey was not an easy one for Mr. & Mrs. Dee. It took a lot of time and patience. It took a lot of observing and learning about their mother's world and her way of thinking. It was through learning about her mother's weaknesses that they found their way to success.

Their mother was very afraid of rain storms. One evening Mrs. Dee stopped in to visit her mother during a storm and found her mother curled up in a closet shaking with fear from the thunder. This was it! The key they had been looking for. Mr. & Mrs. Dee started to convince their mother that she would be much safer staying with them for a while. Her home needed repairs and the repairs could be completed during that time. At first, she refused. Then Mr. & Mrs. Dee noticed a house a few doors away from them was up for sale. They convinced their mother to come and look at it. For the moment, her mother was willing to picture herself in another house very close to her daughter temporarily. It took another frightful storm to get her to actually consider leaving, but she agreed to go. Mrs. Dee was very relieved at this point. She had finally succeeded at getting her mother out of a very unsafe and unhealthy situation, without having to cause great stress on an already stressful situation. While awaiting bank approval for that new house, Mrs. Dee's mother moved in with her and her husband. She adjusted to her new surroundings quicker and easier than expected. It is very possible, that those moments of terror her daughter caught glimpses of during those storms, perhaps were happening more frequently than thought during those nights she lived alone. Once in her daughter and son-in-law's home, she found this new form of security to be something she could live with after all! Mrs. Dee hired part-time caregivers to come into their home. This allowed her time to continue to work at her job, and most importantly, time for her and her husband to enjoy well-deserved "date nights" together. As time went on, it turned out that her mother's journey ended unexpectedly due to a COVID pneumonia. She never made it to the final stage of dementia but was able to remain in her daughter's home with her family until the end. Although Mrs. Dee is currently going through a grieving period with the loss of her mother, she finds strength in knowing that although her family went through some very trying times together, many warm and wonderful memories were made as they shared those last challenging yet loving years together in the comfort of their home.

There is no doubt about it, the caregiving journey becomes very rocky, uncomfortable, and treacherous when a loved one who has been living alone develops dementia. It is not easy to remove them from an environment they are accustomed to or to try to convince them that a safer place is better for their own good. Many caregivers are faced with this and go through this experience with a lot of anxiety and pain trying to find the right solutions.

Stage 6: Moderately severe Alzheimer's disease. At this stage, the ability to perform even basic activities of daily life becomes difficult. They begin to require assistance in putting on their clothing properly. Unless supervised, they may put clothing on backward, may have difficulty putting their arm in the correct sleeve, or may dress in the wrong sequence placing underwear over their long pants.

Bathing deficits become apparent. They have difficulty adjusting the temperature of the bath water, become unable to bathe independently, and require assistance dressing and undressing. They generally develop personal hygiene problems including properly brushing their teeth.

Unless supervised, they have difficulty managing toileting. They may place the toilet tissue in the wrong place and may forget to flush the toilet properly. Urinary incontinence begins. It usually starts with an occasional accident, then progresses to more frequent occurrences. This can often be managed or even prevented initially with frequent toileting. Helpful strategies for managing incontinence include appropriate bed pads, absorbent undergarments, and/or disposable underwear. Fecal incontinence begins. This normally occurs after urinary incontinence. If fecal incontinence occurs first, it is usually a result of an underlying Gastro-Intestinal problem and not dementia.

Cognitive deficits are so great in this stage it is often referred to as the "Velcro Stage". At this point in time, the person often experiences such feelings as: "I don't know what I just did, I don't know what I'm supposed to do next". They experience feelings of being so lost and insecure, that they tend to want to stick to the caregiver as much as possible. They know that their caregiver knows what to do next, and will guide them throughout their day. They often become very stressed when their caregiver is out of sight. Toward the end of this stage, much direction is often required to keep them content. They may begin to fidget, pace, move objects around, and place items where they may not belong. Other forms of purposeless or inappropriate actions may occur due to fear and frustration. More information about dealing with difficult behaviors will be discussed in future parts of this journey.

For caregivers unable to build a strong enough support system, or for those whose loved one's condition just gets too tough to handle, or for caregivers whose own health becomes too frail to handle this enormous task, placement is sometimes necessary.

Meet Mr. P. He and his wife had a great life and marriage together. They never had children but were both athletic and loved the outdoors surrounded by nature. They enjoyed the company of others and kept in close contact with a large number of friends. As they neared retirement age, it became obvious that Mrs. P's abilities were slipping. She was becoming forgetful and confused. They both made the best of it and managed to simplify their lives to meet their needs as her stages of dementia progressed. Although Mr. P. had a medical background he remained open to learning and obtaining as much medical information about dementia as possible. He had very little difficulty retraining his brain to understand and accept the changes his wife was exhibiting throughout this journey. However, despite all of this, one day it became obvious to him, that her constant need for his full attention the entire time they were together became more than he could bare. He decided to try taking a few days and then an occasional week-long respite time off while Mrs. P stayed with paid caregivers that she seemed content with. He found that his wife seemed to do fine while he was away. Of course, she would ask for him, but her time concept was off, and she was unsure of how long he'd been gone. After experiencing several respite times away, he felt that when he returned, her demand for his constant attention continued to be more than he could give her. It was time to increase his team and try permanent placement. He discovered that long-term placement was not an easy decision to make. After carefully researching, he found an Assisted Living that he felt met the needs of both him and his wife. He spoke to the Director and met with the staff who were more than happy to answer all of his questions. He felt relief in knowing that this choice seemed best suited for his wife. Mrs. P. began making friends from the time she got there. However, she still went through an adjustment period of being in a new home for several months afterward. Mr. P. continues to visit often. Due to her lack of time concept, she often feels he is living there with her. When he's gone, she feels he is at work. Both Mr. & Mrs. P are now adjusting well to this new way of life. Mr. P. will be the first to admit, that placement is not as easy as it sounds. You are still a caregiver even after the placement of your loved one. There have been several times when Mr. P. was called on in the middle of the night when his wife developed a medical condition or tripped and fell. He would go and meet her at the hospital. He found that involving Hospice in her care helped eliminate some of those late-night trips, as she could be seen by a Hospice Nurse in her Memory Care Center rather than having to be transported to the emergency room. There are still times when she asks "Will we ever be able to go home again?" Where feelings of guilt and depression start to come over him. The roads continue to be challenging at times, but through education and brain retraining, both of their journeys are becoming less anxiety-ridden and more content and peaceful. Although they are no longer residing under one roof, they are still able to continue building memorable happy moments during their times together once again in spite of it.

Meet Mr. Tee and his wife in late stage 6. Prior to retraining his brain, Mr. Tee was caregiving alone for his wife and felt overwhelmed with the amount of time and care she required. She refused to let him help her with just about anything, including bathing and most incontinence care. She refused to get into the car with him when it was time to take her to a doctor's appointment, or anywhere else for that matter. Mr. Tee began taking dementia training and became a member of a support team. At first, he stated, "This is too much, I just don't think I can handle this." Once he learned to retrain his brain and took the initiative to ask for and get more help, things began to change. It was determined that because his wife's thinking abilities were back in time, there was a good chance that her resistance to allowing him to take part in her personal care stemmed from the fact that he was a man. Young girls aren't supposed to undress in front of grown men! Sure enough, Mr. Tee hired a female caregiver to assist with his wife's personal care. She allowed her caregiver to bathe her without hesitation! She even went willingly into the car with her without a fuss. It is amazing to see the difference in both Mr. Tee and his wife now. You'll be surprised by his replies, as we pass by and ask how he is doing today. "Hello Mr. Tee, how are you and your wife doing today?" "Things are going o.k. I've got this handled. She paces back and forth in our hallway and living room throughout the day, but I'm all right with that. As long as she can see me or her caregiver, she's content. And that makes me feel content too. Don't get me wrong, I have to hide anything of importance or it disappears. And she goes through several rolls of toilet tissue a day, but I've learned to deal with it, and not sweat the small stuff. She can't help it. Sure, there may be times when it gets a little tough, I'm not going to lie to you, but all in all, I can't complain. I have managed to find good dependable help. Now I am able to go out and get in a round of golf now and then with my friends. That really helps recharge me. One thing I do miss is the ability to carry on a good conversation with her. I look forward to meeting up with my golf friends and support group friends to fill in that part of my needs. They have become like family to me."

Mr. Tee's wife has been showing signs of dementia for several years. He has "plan B" in place when things begin to get worse. A new Assisted Living is being built near their home. He is feeling that his wife may one day require even more care or may benefit from the increased activities and socialization that this new Assisted Living may offer. Since it is so close to their home, he will still be able to spend a lot of time with her, yet have a greater team of assistants on their side when that time comes.

Stage 7: Severe Alzheimer's disease also known as the **Failure to Thrive stage**. Early in this stage, speech becomes limited to approximately a half-dozen or fewer intelligible words. As this stage progresses, speech becomes even more limited (expressive aphasia) to at most, a single intelligible word. The person may also develop receptive aphasia as well. The words they hear no longer make sense to them. Caregivers sometimes mistake this for hearing loss, when in reality, they hear the words, but they seem like a foreign language to them. Once speech is lost, the ability to ambulate independently (without assistance), becomes lost. With enough physical care and guidance provided in the early seventh stage, loss of ambulation can potentially be postponed. Loss of the ability to ambulate independently is followed by the loss of the ability to sit up independently. They may lean and fall over when seated unless there are armrests to hold them up in the chair.

    I would like to introduce you to Dot. She has recently traveled on this journey with her husband Joe. Joe was a very intelligent, kind, and caring husband who began showing signs of cognitive decline about 5 years ago. Although not easy, he and his wife managed to make the best of each stage of his illness. Due to cognitive decline, he lost his managerial job. At this point, he was still able to find other types of jobs that required less detail, and was able to work for another year in these areas. Dot was also employed part-time. Their journey together was often met with many detours. Joe's physical abilities began to decline as well. At first, he began to drag his foot when walking, his gait became unsteady. Before long, he was diagnosed with Lewy Body dementia, with Parkinson's disease. The 2-story home they were living in had too many steps to climb and required more upkeep than they were able to manage. They soon learned to problem-solve each step of the way. They sold their home and moved into a smaller, more manageable one-story home. They planned ahead and adapted their new home to accommodate all types of disabilities including fall risk safety features and wheelchair access ability. Together, they were able to remain in a community setting and soon became friends with very caring and helpful neighbors. At this point in time, Joe was no longer able to work but did attend special physical therapy exercise classes and programs. His condition continued to deteriorate at a fast pace. His balance and loss of muscle control resulted in numerous falls. He began using a special walker designed for Parkinson's disease. Before long, he was confined to a wheelchair. Despite all of these declines, he and his wife were able to continue to attend and enjoy time in movie theaters as well as meet with friends for dinner or coffee socials.

Their son moved into the home to help out. Before long, the family's support system had grown to include a Hospice nurse, a Case Manager, a Home care assistant, a physical therapist, and a massage therapist. Joe was now sleeping in a hospital bed which was situated in the grand room of the house where he enjoyed looking out at the backyard through their big picture windows. His abilities continued to fade fast. Despite physical therapy, his muscle weakness increased. It often took 2 people to assist him out of bed and into his wheelchair. Nonetheless, he and Dot and their son were able to share quality time together. If Joe's condition caused him to become upset or angry, they proacted rather than reacted. They allowed him to vent, and were able to de-escalate his anger and frustrations. Before long, that anger was replaced by laughter and joy. They learned to make the best of even the toughest situations. Even Joe's dog remained loyal to him and stayed by his side through thick and thin. Joe's appetite and thirst soon faded away. He grew weaker by the day. He was often up at night and in his increased confusion, he would attempt to get out of bed. Dot knew this would be unsafe as he was too weak to hold himself up and would likely fall again. Unfortunately, Dot's sleep was often minimal at this point in time. To compensate, she and her son would take turns staying up at night with Joe. To help calm him, Dot often spent time reading to Joe shorter and shorter stories from picture books she found in the local library. Although these times were very difficult, this part of the journey is usually the shortest lasting. Joe slowly stopped eating altogether. The Hospice nurse convinced the family his days were limited and they agreed to have Joe transported to the local Hospice facility where he could be made more comfortable. This also would allow the family time to get a little more rest. Dot continued to stay with Joe at this facility all hours of the day or night. She was encouraged by the Hospice nurses to spend at least some nights at home to catch up on much-needed rest. Family and friends were able to stop in and visit. Joe was surrounded by soft music and pleasant aromatherapy every evening. Joe's immobility at this point seemed to be causing him pain and discomfort. The nurses kept a close monitor on this and provided repositioning and medication to help keep him comfortable.10 days later, Joe passed away. Their dementia journey had ended. However, those memories of the good times they shared together would live on. This journey was not easy for Joe's family, but through it all, they managed to find peace and make wonderful memories of the quality time spent together in spite of it.

TRAIL MARKER 6. THROUGH THE ROUGH TERRAIN

Learning to deal with Difficult Challenges

Now that we have climbed Mount Education and descended the Stages, we find ourselves packed with medical and psychological information, our own life experiences, as well as the experiences of other caregivers, we proceed ahead. As you have learned, the Caregiving journey is not for the weak of heart. It is an ongoing process of building patience, understanding, acceptance, endurance, nurturing, and empowerment. It involves promoting purpose and meaning back into your daily lives. It involves asking for and ensuring you have a strong base of assistance and support to ensure your own well-being as well as the person being cared for. Most days are filled with challenges. It is through mastering these challenges, sometimes through problem-solving, sometimes a mood enhancement medication may be necessary, and sometimes just learning to let it go, that we reach our goal of peace and contentment.

We want to keep in mind, as humans, we have a strong desire to maintain control of our lives. Aging in itself starts to interfere with that control as the body starts to slow down, and in many cases, breakdown as arthritis, and other health conditions may start to set in. In the world of dementia, one experiences even greater losses as short-term memory fades and with time, many other areas of brain functioning start to diminish. Some of the unwanted behaviors you may encounter with your loved one may be the result of the caregiver feeling the need to take control. This causes the loved one to resist in an effort to hold on to that control.

As we saw earlier with Mrs. D's mother; by stage 5, it becomes unsafe for a person with dementia to live alone in their own home without help. However, the parent wanting to maintain control of their life, often refuses to leave their home, allow anyone to move in with them, or move to an Assisted Living Facility. And so, the challenge begins. According to David Solie in his book "How to say it to Seniors" "Closing the Communication Gap with Our Elders," when safely possible, we need to respect their decision and refocus our energies. Energy should focus on getting them temporary help to meet their needs. This may consist of hiring a housekeeper, a maintenance person, etc. He goes on to say "When we sense resistance to the idea of moving, drop the subject entirely and instead bring the house to life." In other words, allow the person to express all of their past memories and experiences they can recall about the house. Allow them to express their legacy. He then states "Don't mention moving until they bring up the subject again". "Once they have fully expressed the home's meaning and legacy, their need for connection with the physical space will disappear."

I have also found that some caregivers have been successful at getting their loved ones to change their minds about wanting to move or at least allow someone to move in with them; if they catch the conversation, at a time when the person experiences a frightening episode such as was the case with Mrs. D.'s mother who was afraid of being alone during a thunderstorm. Others may get fearful having heard suspicious sounds at night that may have frightened them. This may be enough to convince them that living alone is no longer the ideal situation to be in.

Try to allow the person to maintain as much control of their life as possible. Another way we can do this is by offering them choices whenever possible. However, we never want to offer them a choice where we can't take "no" for an answer. Example: if you find they are very soiled and in need of a bath, you want to avoid the choice of "Would you like to take a bath now?" If they answer "No", you are stuck with that decision. Instead, offer them a choice such as "Would you like this soap or this soap"? Usually offering only 2 choices at a time works best as too many choices can become too confusing. You will know when even 2 choices become too difficult when they continuously answer "I don't know, you choose".

With this in mind, we move forward and seek ideas on how to help prevent as well as handle episodes of difficult challenges and behaviors. Not everyone who develops dementia becomes angry and aggressive. Many caregivers express this fear when they first experience the changes and confusion in their loved ones. By reflecting on your own life, you may be able to recall times when you became so frustrated or angry that you said things you wished you would not have said. You may have found yourself raising your voice in anger. You may have even found yourself in that same anger situation in the present. You regret this type of behavior, but you are only human. The stress and anxiety have built up inside and taken over like a pressure cooker. The buildup of steam needs to come out. Perhaps once you let that anger out, you felt both relieved and guilty at the same time. It is natural to build up frustration, anxiety, and anger when constantly faced with annoying and unpleasant situations. Understanding why these annoying situations are happening, and learning to retrain your brain to **proact rather than react** to the situation will slowly help prevent or at least help one deal with the anger and frustration in a more acceptable way. In retraining, we remind ourselves that the annoying behavior coming from the person with dementia is not intentional. This is brain damage taking over. In most cases, they are not aware of what they just said or did to upset you. It helps to envision an imaginary, clear shield in front of you. When your loved one says or does something to annoy you, let it go, let it bounce off of that shield, and not reach your heart. What you are hearing or seeing is not something they would normally say or do if they did not have a brain disease.

If that does not work for you, try to leave the area if able, and let off the steam somewhere else. If unable to leave the house and go for a walk, perhaps locking yourself into the bathroom for a few minutes will work. If feelings of sadness take over rather than anger, the same holds true. Try to find a place where you can be alone or at least away from your loved one and allow yourself to cry until those negative feelings and emotions pass. Talking to someone in your support team who understands what you are going through can also be very helpful. Anger is often a way of your body telling you – "I need a break". Learn to be kind to yourself, and find a way to get the help you need so that you can take that much-needed break. It allows your body time to relax and recharge.

A person experiencing dementia may also get frustrated, angry, and upset – rightly so. It is very frustrating when one finds themselves unable to tackle what used to be the simplest tasks or to communicate in a way that others can understand as they did before dementia appeared. Most of this frustration and anger, if caught early, can be minimized with caregiver intervention, and behavior modification. This prevents that "pressure cooker" effect. Dementias involving the frontal lobe of the brain in early stages, such as in Lewy Body and Frontal Temporal Lobe dementia may require both behavior modification and medical intervention to curb the anxiety.

The brain controls our thoughts and behaviors. When certain areas become damaged by these diseases, thought processes can get very obscured. If you have ever woken from a strange and crazy dream far-fetched from reality and wondered how your brain could ever have devised such weird thoughts, you may get a little picture of what may be going on in the minds of some people afflicted by dementia. They may be experiencing "awake dreams" as they verbally express hallucinations, paranoia, or delusional actions.

With Dementia, Behavioral problems are sometimes categorized into 3 Main Types:

Thoughts, Emotions, and Behaviors.

1. **Thought disturbances** can result from language difficulties, comprehension difficulties, delusions, paranoia, or hallucinations.
2. **Emotional difficulties** may appear due to agitation, anxiety, and/or depression
3. **Functional-behavioral changes** may include problems with aggression, wandering, repeating, altered sleep patterns, or excessive desire for sexual relations

It is important to remember that behavior is a form of communication. Also, disturbing, unwanted behavior is often disturbing to caregivers – not to the person with dementia. They do not recall ever displaying the behavior and therefore deny ever saying or doing what they are being "accused" of! Scolding them to try to correct the behavior does not work. "I did not say (or do) that". "I would never say (do) that. "How could you say that about me?" They truly do not recall their negative behavior.

In the case of dementia, for the negative behavior to be modified, educating caregivers rather than treating the person is crucial to behavioral therapy.

Caregiver Education is based on the following areas:

- Learning what to expect: how brain damage changes a person's abilities including recall, understanding, reason and judgement
- Learning to catch and address your loved one's behavioral uneasiness early before it escalates.
- Learning problem solving strategies
- Learning ways to decrease anxiety and stress
- Learning ways of positive communication including the importance of positive body language
- Learning ways of positive interactions
- Learning supportive interaction
- Improving caregiver relationships
- Finding ways to bring joy to your life and the life of your loved one

Ways to Promote Positive Communication:

We have already learned many ways damage to the brain changes behavior. You have met caregivers who have learned to deal with and make the best of their loved one's dementia changes.

Let's walk ahead now, and explore ways we can learn to communicate more positively with someone experiencing a brain disease.

Expect repetition. It is inevitable when someone has no recollection of what they've just said or done you will hear their stories repeated again and again. Master ways to deal with it so that it does not upset you. When your loved one starts to ask the same question, it is sometimes helpful to answer and send the question back to them: "I'm not sure, what do you think about it? "This may break their questioning as it requires an answer from them instead. Even if they respond with "I don't know, that's why I asked you" you can keep it positive by smiling and saying something like "Then I guess we both have some research to do! "Then change the topic or put on some pleasant music such as an old-time sing-a-long tune to take a break from the repetitiveness that may be troubling to you. Try to keep things positive.

Avoid the negatives – No one likes to be told what to do. This is especially true of someone with dementia. Although the caregiver needs to monitor safety and provide assistance when needed, it is important to learn to do this in a positive way whenever possible. When it comes to positive communication, it is important to learn to avoid negative words that sound as if we are taking control. The disease has already taken away some of your loved one's ability to control their life the way they were accustomed. It is only natural that they want to hold on to as much control as possible. To help them through this, it is important that the caregiver **eliminate direct commands as well as the words "No", "Don't", "You Can't", "Stop That"** etc. from your vocabulary. Telling a person who is trying to maintain control of their life that they can't do something will only get you an opposite response "Oh Yea, Watch Me!"

Instead, we learn to validate, give them a reason why this isn't working at the time, and distract them. **Validation** shows you believe them, and understand the action they are attempting to accomplish. it sends a positive message that you are on their side and ready to assist.

Problem-Solving provides a fix to the situation.

Distraction takes their thoughts away from that action and on to a more acceptable one.

An example of this is: If in the middle of the night you find your loved one trying to go out the door for a walk and fidgeting with the lock, instead of saying "No, you can't go out there now"; a caregiver might say, "I can see you are ready to go for a walk" (<u>Validation</u>) "That darn door lock is broken again. I have the repair man coming in the morning to fix it. (<u>Problem-Solving</u>) Don't worry, it's under warranty". (Adding about the warranty may keep him/her from trying to fix it them self).

"Until the repair man gets here, let's go have a cup of hot chocolate (or whatever their favorite beverage or snack).You can tell me about all of those great trophies of yours and how you won them. I love those stories." (<u>Distraction</u>)

We often refer to made-up, problem-solving excuses as "Therapeutic Fibbing". Some caregivers find it hard to use this method. This type of "Fibbing" is not intended to take advantage of your loved one. Instead, it is a method used to solve their problem therapeutically before their frustration escalates.

Avoid "butting heads". There is no convincing someone with dementia that they are wrong. They are in a state of a different reality. In this reality, **they are always right**. They are unable to get into our world of reality, we must learn to get into theirs. Trying to convince them otherwise is futile. So instead of finding yourself in a situation where your conversation is going back and forth "Yes, it is", "No it isn't", your response works best when kept positive: "Oh, that's interesting" – "I never knew that". Now instead of starting a battle, you've uplifted their self-esteem. You may even find it interesting to let them continue their story and learn more about their dementia world – "Tell me more" …

In cases where your loved one flatly refuses to do something you want them to do – such as refusing to get into the car when you need to go somewhere: this most likely may be due to the fact that they want to take control of their own situation. Staying positive and getting creative by finding ways to allow them to feel a part of the decision instead of forcing them into the car may help eliminate negative behavior. For example, if they say, "I'm not getting in to that car" responding in a non-threatening curious voice "Well I thought about walking but it's so far to go; do you think we can make it on foot?" Now you are placing the control back into their hands. (Even though you know that walking is not a real option due to the distance) you may be able to convince them that the distance and weather may influence his/her decision. You may also try "Is there something wrong with the car? Should we take in to have it checked out?" Or if he or she is very frugal you may continue with "How about we go and look at the new cars they have out on the market?"

What we are really trying to accomplish is to find ways to reach our goal while helping them feel a sense of control.

Catch it Early – If you find your loved one is irritated by something, perhaps they are looking for something and unable to find it, try to assist right away. If ignored, frustration and irritation will escalate into agitation, which will continue to escalate into unwanted behaviors that for some, can result in violence. At the first sign of frustration, intervene and validate. "I can see you are looking for something dear, is there something I can help you with". **Don't react** to any negative comments they may let out, (use that clear shield!) instead **proact.** They may already be very frustrated and need to vent and let it out. Allow them to do so verbally without taking it to heart. Accept any negative comments as a reward that you were able to allow them to release some of that steam. Remain calm, and positive, and remember, they are in a different reality. Since they are unable to recall where they put something, they may accuse you or someone else who had been in the house, of stealing the item that is lost. "My purse is gone; I think Susie stole it". Or they may even accuse you of having stolen it. Instead of reacting to the accusation, continue to proact. **Validate and focus on solving the problem,** not the accusation. For instance: "Is that purse missing again? Here, let me see if I can help you find it." If you are not successful after looking for it for a while, go on to **distraction.** "It looks like it's lunchtime already. Let's go eat, and we'll come back and look for that purse later. It'll give us more time to think about where it can be. "During lunch, come up with another activity that will take her thoughts away from the missing object.

Catching frustration early and resolving the problem, **helps prevent the sparks from turning into a bonfire.**

To promote feelings of peace and harmony, when communicating with a person with dementia, it is important to try to **communicate in a calm, caring, positive manner;** as well as a soft, comforting tone of voice. Learn to adapt to his/her way of communicating. It is important not to rush them through their explanations or force them to try to understand your way of communicating. Try holding their hand. Hugs and hand holding can be comforting for most.

Body language is understood long after the spoken language diminishes. Many times, caregivers have approached me, with their loved one at their side, saying something to the effect of: "This is getting to be too much. You wouldn't believe what we went through this morning. I don't know what I'm going to do with him/her …".When asked to come to my office so we could talk about this alone, they often reply: "Oh don't worry, he/she can't understand a word I'm saying". This is an example of where knowledge is power. Once a caregiver is educated in the area of the power of tone of voice and body language, they become enlightened and learn to respect this form of communication. They learn to use it in a therapeutic way. Loved ones who have lost the ability to communicate through language (expressive and receptive aphasia) are still able to understand and are often tuned in more closely to the tone of voice and body language. Without realizing it, the caregiver's anxiety in their voice, their glances, and hand gestures toward their loved one send the signal that he/she is upset with me. I did something wrong. I am a bad person. I am a burden. etc.…

Take this time to study your actions or the actions of another with your ears blocked from the sound. As suggested during the early part of this journey, try turning on a television show with the volume off. See if you can determine what the person is trying to convey and how they are feeling. Without even realizing it, a lot of information is expressed through our body language. Even when words are lost or jumbled, a person with dementia is able to pick up on these gestures and expressions.

As mentioned earlier, another important point to keep in mind, is that a person with dementia often mirrors our behavior. If we walk into a room angry, or in a bad mood, they are apt to pick up on that and become angry or upset themselves. On the other hand, if we remain in a good mood and smile, (even if you are not feeling that way inside at the time), those positive feelings and support will usually rub off on them and help turn things around in a more positive direction – toward peace and harmony.

Supportive ways of interacting By now, you may already be practicing ways of supportive interactions. These include such things as:

Establishing a routine. Scheduling activities of daily living for the same time and place each day; for example, bathing, dressing, grooming, brushing the teeth, meals, exercise, and fun activities for the day usually promotes a feeling of security to the person with dementia and helps minimize stress. It is sometimes helpful to post an "Activity Board" on the refrigerator or somewhere where it can be easily seen by your loved one. Most people find that a whiteboard works best, as routines, may sometimes change for the day due to appointments or special activities.

When it comes to establishing bathing routines, a daily shower or tub bath is not usually necessary for most people as they age. The skin tends to become drier, there is usually less perspiration. Instead, a simple sink bath in which one wets a washcloth with warm water and mild soap washes and rinses under the arms and the private areas often suffices. On days when showers are planned, it is helpful to look at time limitations. When possible, it is helpful to choose the most relaxed time of the day for bathing and grooming. If bathing can be done the night before an early morning appointment, for instance, it will help avoid anxiety over the need to rush through an otherwise time-consuming routine. This will decrease the stress of worry about making it to the appointment on time.

If your loved one resists or refuses to take a shower This is not an unusual occurrence that caregivers face. It can be caused by a number of things. Is your loved one expected to go into the bathroom alone and take a shower? If so, depending on the stage of dementia they are in, they may or may not be accomplishing the task they say they are doing. We don't always think about this, but taking a shower requires a lot of brain functioning. We have to be aware of the steps to turning the water on to the proper temperature, getting towels, soap, and shampoo ready, having after shower clean clothing ready to put on, undressing and removing any jewelry if applicable, then getting into the shower, soaping up, rinsing, washing hair, etc.As dementia progresses, one loses the ability to organize their thoughts and sequence them. Short-term memory loss also plays a factor in this. Did I already soap up, did I wash my hair yet? They may end up stepping into the shower, possibly under cold running water, get slightly wet, and step out again. There may be a chance they never stepped into the shower at all! Once a caregiver takes on the responsibility of assisting with the shower, there is a good chance your loved one resists or refuses to take a shower. If this occurs, it is often helpful to look closely at when the resistance occurs. Is it at a mention of the words or thought of shower or bath? Does the resistance start when trying to enter the bathroom or the shower? Does it occur when first undressing? When first hearing the water turned on? These observations can give you a clue as to what may be causing the anxiety. Now let's look back into those younger childhood experiences. What happens when young children first learn to swim or take a shower? They rarely like to get their head wet or get water in their face. How do most children feel about taking showers after gym class? They rarely like to get undressed in front of others. Your loved one with dementia views life as if they were back in time. Thus, it is not surprising that a shower for them may be looked upon as a very anxiety-provoking experience. If your loved one has difficulty with balance or has had falls in the past, this too may add to the fear of stepping into a wet, slippery area. Some helpful hints:

Use Contrasting colors in the bathroom. A white floor, white sink, toilet, and shower may all appear to look like one big cloud to someone with dementia. Have a contrasting color, nonskid floor mat in and out of the shower. If the shower matches the bathroom walls, you may need to introduce something of color in and around the shower to define the walls. Avoid dark solid color mats like black or brown on the floor as they may be perceived as a hole in the floor and they may try to step over or around it.

Make sure your bathroom is safe and pleasant to the eyes. Keep the room free of clutter with good lighting, nonskid flooring or mats, and secure grab bars. Soothing pictures may add a feeling of warmth and welcome.

Always have your loved one sit when getting undressed, dressed, or showering. They should never have to raise one leg when attempting to put pants on or take them off. This is a dangerous habit, as it tends to throw one's balance off. **Shower chairs** with side handles seem to work best. **Grab bars** when properly installed, are also important ways to help relieve the fear of falling and avoid falls.

Towel wraps work well for modesty. If your loved one seems uncomfortable undressing in front of their caregiver, a long bath towel can be used to wrap around them and tuck in at the top. Some stores sell these with a Velcro tab to keep them intact. As the person showers, the wrap can get wet, and soap can be applied to it as a type of wrap-around washcloth. After the shower, a dry towel can be brought in and the wet one slipped off as the dry one is placed over top. If this is completed while still sitting in the shower, it will avoid any water getting onto the bathroom floor as well as maintain privacy and dignity.

Hand-held Showers usually work best. A hand-held shower can allow you to start the shower in the opposite way most of us are accustomed to – start with the feet first. This allows your loved one to get used to the water temperature and keeps the water away from the face until last.

Driving: When it comes to a person with dementia being behind the wheel, I find myself trying to convince the caregiver, if able, to start offering to take over this responsibility. It is not always easy for a person with dementia to give up this part of their life. Some people realize it is too confusing for them, and give it up on their own. Others may insist that they are still very proficient at it. If you compare the effects of alcohol vs dementia on driving: In Florida for men, it only takes 2 to 3 drinks to be at or above the legal limit of 0.08 depending on body weight, metabolism, when they ate last to be able to drive safely. For women, it usually only takes 2 drinks to reach the legal limit in Florida. This amount of alcohol is proven to have the following effects on a person: A decline in concentration, short-term memory loss, lack of speed control, reduced information processing capability, and impaired perception.

A person with brain damage caused by a dementing illness experience most of those declines all of the time - without alcohol! Driving is unsafe for them as well as for passengers in the car and others on the road including bicyclists and pedestrians crossing the street. As you recall, they experience loss of peripheral and 3D vision as well as abilities to problem solve and sequence.

Driving tests are available to test these skills if your loved one flatly refuses to quit. You may also contact the Department of Motor Vehicles to get a form that states that your loved one who is still driving has dementia. You can mail this form back to them and remain anonymous. It usually takes about 3 months for a reply, but your loved one will receive a letter in the mail, stating they are required to take and pass a driving test or their driver's license will be revoked. At this point, many drivers are willing to give up driving rather than take another test. However, that option is available to them.

Caregiver Strategies:

As safety permits, encourage your loved one to do as much for themselves as safely possible. This will help to promote a sense of independence and accomplishment. Look for things they are still capable of doing.

Try to keep your Loved one Content – Focus on their present abilities. Try to find "busy work" for them to do that can bring them a feeling of importance and accomplishment. A few simple ideas might be:

Laundry: folding towels, washcloths, or other items if capable

Sorting: tools, nuts & bolts, or other objects your loved one may be interested in (make sure they are not something they may put in their mouth and choke on)

Planting & Watering flowers

Sweeping the floor or outdoor areas

Dusting, vacuuming

Painting with watercolors or washable paint

Adult Coloring pages are often fun to do; using soft leaded colored pencils also works well with these

Unfinished wood objects to sand, and paint, can be purchased at dollar stores, department stores, or craft stores

Cards: If they are still able to play games such as solitaire or war, these can keep them busy while having fun. Counting a deck of cards to see if they are all in the pack; sorting them according to suits (spades, diamonds, etc.). Mix 2 decks with different designs on the back, and have them sort them apart.

Puzzles – Start simple with 50 or fewer pieces. If this is too difficult, larger and fewer-piece puzzles can be introduced. For those in later stages, wooden puzzles with 6 or 12 pieces may work, especially those that have a theme that may be acceptable for adults such as animals, plants, or food.

Improvement in Caregiver Relationships Get to know and accept your loved one's imperfections and loss of abilities; then focus on their remaining abilities at this moment in time. Try to make the most of these. Everyone needs to feel useful and important.

Although you may not always feel this positive, try to smile, remain calm and use a "best friend" approach. This builds a warm sense of comradery and an "I am here for you" feeling that helps decrease anxiety for both of you. This also gives the caregiver a sense of pride for the wonderful way you are able to help your loved one who is facing this debilitating disease. Find pride in the way you are able to positively manage this life-changing situation in spite of it.

When behavior modification strategies are not enough When unwanted behavior is noticed, be sure to check for underlying causes of the behavioral changes such as infection, discomfort, hunger, thirst, injury, pain, or a need to use the bathroom.

Also, check to see if this behavior may be a result of a medication that can potentially cause agitation such as an OTC sleep agent, a bladder-control medication, a dopaminergic drug used to treat Parkinson's disease.

In most cases, behavior modification works well. However, for some despite all of the positive efforts to maintain peace and contentment, a person's behavior may not respond as we had hoped. If these efforts fail, and the person's behavior either shows signs of continued depression, or anxiety and anger become a threat to himself or others, medication may be necessary.

A Licensed physician or Licensed Nurse Practitioner can prescribe medications. Please be aware that the medications listed below are not being recommended, but rather are listed to give you a better understanding of what prescription drugs are available at this time; in case your loved one's physician prescribes one or more of them. Also note that the field of medicine is advancing at a fast pace. Therefore, there is a good chance that new medications as well as information on the ones listed may have changed since this information was put to pen. You can be assured that the latest information, precautions, and side effects will be listed in the handout accompanying the prescription. If you are unable to locate it, your pharmacist can provide one for you.

<u>Antidepressants</u> are usually safe and effective, with minimal side effects. Results usually appear within just a few weeks. (However, as with all medications, be sure to read the insert instructions for information on side effects and adverse reactions to watch for.)

Selective serotonin reuptake inhibitors (SSRIs) are the most common type used for Alzheimer's disease. These are a newer class of antidepressant medications. Their generic or chemical names are listed followed by available brand names in parentheses: Citalopram (**Celexa**), Escitalopram (**Lexapro**), Fluoxetine (**Prozac**), Paroxetine (**Paxil**, Paxil CR), and Sertraline (**Zoloft**).

Antidepressants that inhibit the reuptake of brain chemicals other than serotonin include venlafaxine (Effexor), mirtazapine (Remeron), and bupropion (Wellbutrin).

Tricyclic antidepressants, such as amitriptyline (Elavil), nortriptyline (Pamelor), and desipramine (Norpramine), **are no longer used as first-choice treatments**. However, they may be prescribed if other medications aren't effective. The **tricyclic** antidepressant amitriptyline (**Elavil**), can cause sedation. These drugs also **can react with** the medicines used to treat Alzheimer's, including rivastigmine (**Exelon**), donepezil (**Aricept**), and galantamine (**Razadyne**)

For increased anxiety where behavior management and antidepressants are not enough,

<u>**Antianxiety medications**</u> may be prescribed. Here is a list of some of the common ones known as **Benzodiazepines:**

Clonazepam (**Klonopin**), Clorazepate (**Tranxene**), Lorazepam (**Ativan**), and Diazepam(**Valium**)

Benzodiazepines slow down the central nervous system to relieve anxiety and nervousness. **Some drug(s) may interact with them including alcohol, caffeine,** cimetidine, contraceptive or birth control pills, **herbal or dietary supplements such as kava, melatonin, St. John's Wort or**

valerian, isoniazid, medicines for mental problems or psychiatric disturbances, medicines for fungal infections (fluconazole, itraconazole, ketoconazole, voriconazole), medicines for HIV infection or AIDS, nicardipine, prescription **pain medicines,** probenecid, rifampin, rifapentine, or rifabutin, **some antibiotics** (clarithromycin, erythromycin, troleandomycin), **some medicines for colds,** hay fever, or other **allergies, some medicines for high blood pressure or heart-rhythm** problems (amiodarone, diltiazem, verapamil), some medicines for seizures (carbamazepine, phenobarbital, phenytoin, primidone), and theophylline.

Carbamazepine **(Tegretol)** is an anti-seizure drug that stabilizes sodium levels in the brain. When used alone – without a benzodiazepine, it may be used to treat agitation. Some seizure meds may also be used to decrease libido when heightened sexual behavior becomes unmanageable.

High oral doses of **benzodiazepines** used for insomnia or anxiety **can also cause memory impairment**. In addition, the drugs cause a specific deficit in "episodic" memory, the remembering of recent events, the circumstances in which they occurred, and their sequence in time. Treatment is based on the quality of life vs side effects.

When behavior modification, antidepressants, and antianxiety medications are not enough:

Antipsychotics may be prescribed. These are used for the treatment of acute and chronic psychosis. They block dopamine receptors in the brain. In 2023, the FDA-approved the antipsychotic **Rexulti** (brexpiprazole) to treat agitation due to Alzheimer's Disease. Other agents that have often been prescribed are: **Zyprexa, Seroquel, and Risperdal.** Antacids may decrease absorption. People with Lewy Body dementia or Parkinson's with Lewy Body may be very sensitive to antipsychotic neuroleptics. These should only be used when extremely necessary, and for as short of periods of time as necessary; be started on low doses, and monitored very closely for sensitive reactions. Haloperidol should be avoided. (Key Considerations BEFORE Treating Behavioral Disturbances in LBD Treatment Options 2023 Lewy Body Dementia Association, Inc

Rexulti (brexpiprazole)and Seroquel (quetiapine fumarate) are considered atypical **antipsychotic** drugs. **Seroquel** helps restore the balance of neurotransmitters in the brain and may help: decrease hallucinations, improve concentration, promote clearer and more positive thinking, decrease nervousness, and help prevent severe mood swings or decrease their frequency.

It is indicated for the treatment of both: depressive episodes and acute manic episodes associated with bipolar disorder.

Although frequently used, Seroquel, like many other mood-modifying drugs, comes with adverse warnings such as: not recommended for use in the elderly with dementia due to increased risks of stroke, heart failure, diabetes, and pancreatitis. Therefore, this is another situation where quality of life is weighed by risks.

Rexulti is sometimes helpful to treat severe agitation in people with Alzheimer's disease. It should be given as directed and not be given sporadically "as needed". Medications can sometimes have an opposite effect on some patients. It is important to monitor your loved one closely when started on new medications, and to inform the physician immediately of any unintended changes that may occur – such as the agitation getting worse instead of better, or other negative behaviors or responses noted.

TRAIL MARKER 7
LEARNING TO BE KIND TO YOURSELF

Finding Peace and Harmony

How strong is your support system? Having a planned routine is not only important for your loved one, it is also important for you. It is important for you as a caregiver to have set days and times set aside as "me time" for yourself. Knowing that you have someone coming in to relieve you every Tuesday and Friday for example, helps you plan your own appointments as well as your Bridge, Bingo, or fishing day! Do you have at least 2 reliable and caring people whom your loved one is comfortable with and who are available to take over and care for him/her to ensure you can have that "me" time? It is not unusual for caregivers to resist asking family or friends for help as they "hate to bother" anyone. On the contrary, taking over the care to give you time off to recharge often proves to be very rewarding to that family member or friend, as they feel an opportunity to play a valuable role in your family's life. It has been scientifically proven that when one takes part in helping another in need, their brain releases mood elevating hormones such as oxytocin. Therefore, rather than feeling as though you are bothering someone when asking for help, realize that you are actually offering them an opportunity to add more good feelings to their life!

If family and friends are not available, hired help is also out there. (See the Medicare.gov link at the end of this chapter for assistance finding a homecare (Home Health) agency near you. Check with your physician, or call a Hospice office, to see if your loved one is a candidate for Palliative or Hospice care at this time. Unlike most illnesses, people with dementia may be able to benefit from Hospice much earlier in their disease process. Hospice may be able to provide some assistance with personal care as well as respite. They also provide access to medical supplies, assistance, and services. If your loved one is a Veteran, they may qualify for VA assistance with Home care, Adult Day Care, and/or financial benefits. When hiring a caregiver through a Home Health Care agency, or independently on your own, be sure to have a written "job description" for them. In other words, have a "to-do" list available and go over it with them before you leave. Although they may have been trained in caring for someone with dementia, this does not mean they can read your mind! It is important they are made aware of the daily routine, as well as what your loved one can and can't do, likes and doesn't like, etc. Having activities planned helps make things run smoother. The caregiver does not have to second guess if it is safe to take your loved one for a walk, take them out in the yard, or even open your refrigerator to give them a snack.

For loved ones who experience separation anxiety, I found that making a short video of yourself, reassuring your loved one that you have only stepped out temporarily, and will be back soon, helps decrease their anxiety. An example of this recording might include: "Hi Honey, I had to run an errand (or go to a doctor's appointment) I will be back soon. Sarah is here with you until I get back. Be sure to make her feel welcome. She is such a wonderful friend. I'm sure you two will have a great time. I'll see you both soon."

I have used Zoom and a laptop computer to record videos such as these in the Adult Day Care setting. Most iPhones will probably work for this as well. If unable to record a video, you may be able to leave a recorded phone message that the caregiver can replay to your loved one once they start asking for or looking for you. Seeing you on the video or hearing your voice message often brings your loved one a sense of relief. This may also prevent them from wandering away trying to find you. It may help to eliminate or at least minimize frequent phone calls that you may otherwise get while away.

I hope by now, you realize what an amazing and wonderful person you are. The precious time you devote to the work you do and the love and devotion you bring to this work of caregiving has not gone unnoticed. You are making a huge impact on your life and the life of your loved one. As you well know, and as I often remind caregivers, life is short. This journey you are on will not last forever. Continue to make the best of each and every day, no matter what situation you find yourself in. When feeling weak, find strength in your support system.

It's true, "There's no place like home. "With the assistance of a strong support team, many families are able to keep their loved ones at home with them throughout this journey. However, if you are unable to build a strong team, there may come a time when you need to look into Assisted Living or Skilled Nursing facilities either for short respite times, or permanent placement. Many a time, a caregiver has asked me, "How do I know when it is time for placement? "My answer is always the same: "It depends on the health and well-being of the caregiver, the status of your loved one, and the strength of your support team". If the caregiver's health is failing and your condition becomes too frail, if the person with dementia's behavior or health becomes too hard to handle, or if outside help is not available or reliable, it's time to look for a new team. The new team is likely one with medical personnel working in shifts, usually found in Assisted Living Facilities with a Memory Support Unit or a Skilled Nursing Facility. If it seems things are heading in that direction, Senior Advisors can be very helpful. These are agents whose services are usually free of charge to the family. They connect with you individually and find out pertinent information needed to help you find a place that works best for you and your loved one, based on distance, the qualities you are looking for, affordability, and your loved one's nursing care requirements. Most agents will accompany you on visits to see each place on your list until you find one that you feel comfortable choosing. Check to see what daily activities are offered by the facility. It is important that your loved one has plenty of things to do to keep him/her content and involved in their new setting. If possible, talk to or at least observe other residents to see if they are content.

If your loved one is placed in a facility, you will find that your job doesn't stop there. You may still find yourself visiting often, accompanying them to doctor's appointments or even having to meet them in an emergency room if they succumb to a fall or injury. Know what to expect. Unlike home, these facilities are not staffed 1:1. Although the facility may offer tender, loving care, the care you are accustomed to at home will be different. However, you will eventually benefit from more undisturbed sleep, and have the support of a team when the care is too much for one to handle alone. It will take time for both of you to adjust to this new way of living. Try to leave any guilt behind. There comes a time in some people's lives when this transition may be necessary. If your loved one is enrolled in Palliative Care or Hospice, they will continue to follow them in the Assisted Living or Skilled Nursing Facility as well.

You now have the tools and the power to make the very best of each and every day no matter what life throws your way. Find peace in knowing that you are mastering the skills of caring for someone with a brain disease. You are making a tremendous difference in their lives by supporting them through the path they are on and helping to make each day content for them. Find peace in knowing that you are not alone on this journey. Keep connecting with your support group friends. Not only will they provide you with the opportunity to vent and discuss your problems, but many caregivers have found valuable community resource information from others in their group as they share privately paid caregivers, Home Health Agency information, Financial Advisors, Legal Assistance, and much more. Many caregivers continue to attend their support group meetings even after their loved one passes. They find it helpful to get through their grieving process with friends they have shared their journey with. They have also discovered that there is no greater reward than the feelings that come from helping another who is struggling and may benefit from what they have learned and experienced.

If you continue to follow what you've learned, then you've reached the part of the trail where peace and harmony begin to prevail. Of course, there will continue to be hard times – there are always hard times in life and in the world, we live in. However, you now have the power and tools to deal with rough times and the ability to find your way back to peace and contentment.

Take time to put some fun back into your life. It is extremely important to remember to reward yourself for all the hard work you are accomplishing. Catch yourself each time you have successfully accomplished your brain retraining. If you find yourself smiling when answering that same question again, then turning the question back to your loved one for their opinion, - catch your good deed. Catch your "Ah Ha, I did it" moments. Feel good about your masteries and reward yourself. Plan and take special enjoyable "me time" for yourself. Many caregivers tend to feel guilty if they go out and enjoy an activity without their loved ones. On the contrary, life without good times and fun leads to depression. It is not helpful to your loved one if you refuse to do this and succumb to depression. It is extremely important for the caregiver to not only ensure their loved one is content but to look at their own life situation as well and make sure you are content. What makes you happy? What brings you joy? What makes you feel content? After answering these questions, be sure to do something about it to make these experiences happen. It is important that you set aside at least 1 to 2 days a week where you can get away and enjoy that "me time" for yourself. Even if this involves hiring a caregiver to take over for you. As mentioned earlier, Adult Day programs can also provide that much-needed respite time for you. You will be amazed at how much these little acts of kindness to yourself help recharge your psyche and take you to the land of inner peace. You are now here. The land of peace and contentment awaits you. To remain in this state, it is important that you practice what you've learned along the way. Remember it takes a team. Use the strong support system you have built to share the load and continue to add joy and happiness to your life. Feel the pride and rewards that come with helping your loved one, and continue to remain in the present instead of looking back. Keep taking one step at a time in the right direction, through this land of Peace and Harmony.

Now that you have walked this walk with me, learned from a few other caregivers with similar experiences, learned to retrain your brain to better understand and adjust more positively to the dementia world, you've mastered the art of caregiving. It is time for me to go, and allow you to continue your work; making the very best of each day, while taking one step at a time.

JOURNEY

Although this book is nearing an end, your journey continues. It is important for you to always realize that you are not alone. The guidance does not stop at the end of this book. There are many organizations here to help. An important one to remember is the Alzheimer's Association and their 24 Hr. Helpline that is available anytime you run into difficult situations or just need someone to talk to for continued professional guidance. Add their number to your contact list:

The phone number for the Alzheimer's Association 24/7 helpline is 800- 272- 3900.

Also note, The Alzheimer's Foundation of America has a 7-day/wk. 9 am to 9 pm helpline: 866-232-8484

I also encourage you to join a caregiver support group (if you are not already attending one).Sharing the caring experience is an important part of this journey. Having the ability to express what you are experiencing as well as enjoying new friendships with others who understand the journey proves very helpful and empowering. For those unable to get away, there are many support groups held over the phone or the internet on Zoom. The Alzheimer's Association and the Alzheimer's Foundation of America, can help you find a support group that works best for you.

If your loved one has a special type of dementia such as Lewy Body or Frontal Temporal Lobe Dementia, each has its own organization that specializes in these areas and often offers support groups and current information on that specific disorder.

- Lewy Body Dementia Association: https://www.lbda.org/;LEWY LINE: 800.539.9767

- Association of Frontal Temporal Degeneration: https://www.theaftd.org/living-with-ftd/newly-diagnosed/ Helpline: 1-866-507-7222

It is my hope that you as a caregiver, realize the importance of the work you are doing, find pride in what you do, and reward yourself. Also, realize the gratefulness your loved one has (even when they are unable to express it); for devoting your time and energy into making their life as happy and content as possible despite their brain injury or disease. This journey won't last forever. Life is short. Continue to make the best of it while you can. You are truly special and have a lot to be proud of.

May peace and contentment be with you always.

JOURNEY'S END. PREPARING FOR THE FINAL JOURNEY HOME.

After your caregiving Journey has ended it is not unusual to feel lost and empty. Caring for your loved one has been a big part of your life. It took up most of your time and energy. There's a great chance those stages of grief will reappear. Finding ways to keep busy, and staying connected with friends (including those in your support group) and family are often helpful. Many caregivers found it helpful to find ways to go out and help others in their community (perhaps taking on a volunteer position in some type of assistance program that interests you). Once again, your local hospice can be very helpful in providing you with grief counseling and support to help you get through your loss.

Unfortunately, there are also many legal matters that need to be taken care of. These can be very stressful times.

This AARP link lists helpful information about those matters that need to be addressed. Many have found this information very helpful:

https://www.aarp.org/home-family/friends-family/info-2020/when-loved-one-dies-checklist.html

HELPFUL REFERENCES FOR THE CARE-GIVING JOURNEY

If you need help finding assistance or information in your area on any of the categories listed below, you may find this Medicare link to be very helpful: https://www.medicare.gov/care-compare/

- Doctors & Clinicians
- Hospitals
- Nursing homes including rehab services
- Home health services
- Hospice care
- Inpatient rehabilitation facilities
- Long-term care hospitals

You can also find local services by contacting Eldercare Locator at 800-677-1116; https://eldercare.acl.gov

For funding assistance and legal information

https://www.nia.nih.gov/health/topics/legal-and-financial-planning

For Medicaid/CHIP or other health insurance options. https://www.medicaid.gov

Find out if you qualify for Social Security disability benefits, contact "compassionate allowances" 800-772-`1213; www.ssa.gov/compassionateallowances

Veterans may contact their local VA office or:

National Association of Veterans and Families (NAVF) Phone: 904-394-3908; https://www.navf.org/

For the uninsured: Visit HealthCare.gov to take a quick screening to help determine your eligibility for the Health Insurance Market.

Many items used for caregiving are tax deductible.

It may be wise to check with AARP: how family caregivers can get the tax breaks they deserve Updated February 7, 2023

https://www.aarp.org/or check with a local tax agent about this.

Learn about driving safety:

www.nia.nih.gov/health/driving-safety-and-alzheimers-disease

Books and organizations that may be of interest to you:

The 36 Hour Day: a family guide to Caring for people who have Alzheimer's Disease and other dementias (a Johns Hopkins Press health book)– August 10, 2021, by Nancy L. Mace (Author), Peter V. Rabins

The Caregiver Help book; Powerful Tools for Caregivers; order at: powerfultoolsforcaregers.org

How to Say It to Seniors; Closing the Communication Gap with Our Elders by David Solie, M.S., P.A

Breaking the habit of being yourself: how to lose your mind and create a new one, February 15, 2013, by Dr. Joe Dispenza

The Alzheimer's and Related Dementias Education and Referral (ADEAR) Center

https://www.nia.nih.gov/health/about-adear-center   800-438-4380

Clinical trials information https://www.alz.org/alzheimers-dementia/research_progress/clinical-trials

OTHER REFERENCES:

5 Steps to Organize Your Loved One's Financial Records, Family Caregiving, Jan. 2013 https://www.aarp.org/caregiving/financial-legal/info-2018/organize-financial-records.html

AARP October/November 2021 **The New Health Heroes** – Life Altering new treatments for heart, mind, and more; **First blood test for Alzheimer's disease.** By Suzanne Schnindler, M.D./ Assistant Professor of Neurology

Alzheimer's Association of America – alz.org/about 1/2023

Alzheimer's Association: Caregiver Health; Grief and Loss as Alzheimer's Progresses 2023

Alzheimer's Society Canada – Frontotemporal dementia, 9/19/2018

Alzforum Theraputics Protollin. Last Updated: 16 Feb 2022. U.S. FDA Status: Alzheimer's Disease (Phase 1) Company: I-MAB Biopharma Co., Ltd., Jiangsu Nhwa Pharmaceutical Co., Ltdhttps://www.alzforum.org/therapeutics/protollin

Fisher Center for Alzheimer's Care Research Foundation the Encyclopedia of Visual Medicine Series an **Atlas of Alzheimer's Disease**, Parthenon, Pearl River (NY) By Barry Reisberg, M.D. **Global Deterioration Scale**, Geriatric Resources Inc., 9/14/2005

http://www.geriatric-resources.com/html/gds.html

Healthline Normopressure Hydrocephalus Written by Lydia Krause Medically reviewed by the University of Illinois-Chicago, College of Medicine on March 22, 2016

NIH National Institute on Aging; www.nia.nih.gov/health/alzheimers/caregiving

National Institute of Neurologic Disorders and Stroke Creutzfeldt-jakob disease fact sheet date last modified: Tue, 2019-08-13 22:02

NHS Causes of Dementia 8 January 2018 **Very well mind**, An Overview of Alcoholic Dementia, Wernicke-Korsakoff Syndrome

By Buddy T, Updated November 19, 2019

Why did Muhammad Ali get dementia? – Heimduo 2023

Made in the USA
Columbia, SC
19 March 2024

36815ea5-c423-4e71-809d-f80ea7e3aef1R02